ISSUES
COMPANION

Death Penalty

Other Books of Related Interest:

Opposing Viewpoints Series

Legal System

Problems with Death

Current Controversies

Capital Punishment

At Issue Series

Does Capital Punishment Deter Crime?

Death Penalty

Uma Kukathas, Book Editor

GREENHAVEN PRESS

An imprint of Thomson Gale, a part of The Thomson Corporation

Detroit • New York • San Francisco • New Haven, Conn. • Waterville, Maine • London

Christine Nasso, *Publisher*
Elizabeth Des Chenes, *Managing Editor*

© 2008 The Gale Group.

For more information, contact:
Greenhaven Press
27500 Drake Rd.
Farmington Hills, MI 48331-3535
Or you can visit our Internet site at http://www.gale.com

ISBN-13: 978-0-7377-3249-8 (hardcover)
ISBN-13: 978-0-7377-3250-4 (pbk.)
ISBN-10: 0-7377-3249-0 (hardcover)
ISBN-10: 0-7377-3250-4 (pbk.)

Library of Congress Control Number: 2007933230

Contents

Foreword   7

Introduction   10

Chapter 1: The Death Penalty in the United States

1. Reevaluating the Death Penalty   20
   Hugo Adam Bedau

2. The Navajo Opt Out of the Death Penalty   34
   Marilyn Berlin Snell

3. The United States Needs to Exercise   43
   Retribution in Considering the Death Penalty
   Robert Blecker

4. Use of the Death Penalty Cannot Be Civilized   57
   Christopher Brauchli

5. Support for the Death Penalty Is Declining   61
   Tony Mauro

6. The Supreme Court May Alter Its Stance   67
   on the Death Penalty
   Benjamin Wittes

Chapter 2: The Death Penalty as a Crime Deterrent

1. Statistical Evidence Shows That the   74
   Death Penalty Is a Deterrent
   Paul H. Rubin

2. The Death Penalty Does Not Deter Crime   80
   Ted Goertzel

3. The Death Penalty Will Not Deter Terrorism   85
   Thomas McDonnell

Chapter 3: Is the Death Penalty Fair?

1. The Unfair Administration of the Death Penalty   **89**
   Dave Lindorff

2. Juvenile Offenders Should Be Eligible   **100**
   for the Death Penalty
   Thomas R. Eddlem

3. Executing the Powerless   **105**
   Michael A. Wolff

4. The Mentally Ill Should Not Be Subject   **109**
   to the Death Penalty
   Sally Satel

5. Age Is Not an Excuse for a Stay of Execution   **113**
   Chuck Klosterman

Chapter 4: Personal Perspectives on the Death Penalty

1. Why I Stopped Supporting the Death Penalty   **119**
   David R. Dow

2. A Chaplain Learns to Forgive Murderers   **124**
   Gary Egeberg

3. The Mother of a Murderer Speaks Out   **129**
   Against the Death Penalty
   Katherine Norgard

4. A Death Row Inmate Reflects on the Justice   **148**
   System and His Time on Death Row
   Amy Goodman and Stanley "Tookie" Williams

Organizations to Contact   **159**

Bibliography   **166**

Index   **171**

Foreword

In the news, on the streets, and in neighborhoods, individuals are confronted with a variety of social problems. Such problems may affect people directly: A young woman may struggle with depression, suspect a friend of having bulimia, or watch a loved one battle cancer. And even the issues that do not directly affect her private life—such as religious cults, domestic violence, or legalized gambling—still impact the larger society in which she lives. Discovering and analyzing the complexities of issues that encompass communal and societal realms as well as the world of personal experience is a valuable educational goal in the modern world.

Effectively addressing social problems requires familiarity with a constantly changing stream of data. Becoming well informed about today's controversies is an intricate process that often involves reading myriad primary and secondary sources, analyzing political debates, weighing various experts' opinions—even listening to firsthand accounts of those directly affected by the issue. For students and general observers, this can be a daunting task because of the sheer volume of information available in books, periodicals, on the evening news, and on the Internet. Researching the consequences of legalized gambling, for example, might entail sifting through congressional testimony on gambling's societal effects, examining private studies on Indian gaming, perusing numerous websites devoted to Internet betting, and reading essays written by lottery winners as well as interviews with recovering compulsive gamblers. Obtaining valuable information can be time-consuming—since it often requires researchers to pore over numerous documents and commentaries before discovering a source relevant to their particular investigation.

Greenhaven's Contemporary Issues Companion series seeks to assist this process of research by providing readers with useful and pertinent information about today's complex issues. Each volume in this anthology series focuses on a topic of current interest, presenting informative and thought-provoking selections written from a wide variety of viewpoints. The readings selected by the editors include such diverse sources as personal accounts and case studies, pertinent factual and statistical articles, and relevant commentaries and over views. This diversity of sources and views, found in every Contemporary Issues Companion, offers readers a broad perspective in one convenient volume.

In addition, each title in the Contemporary Issues Companion series is designed especially for young adults. The selections included in every volume are chosen for their accessibility and are expertly edited in consideration of both the reading and comprehension levels of the audience. The structure of the anthologies also enhances accessibility. An introductory essay places each issue in context and provides helpful facts such as historical background or current statistics and legislation that pertain to the topic. The chapters that follow organize the material and focus on specific aspects of the book's topic. Every essay is introduced by a brief summary of its main points and biographical information about the author. These summaries aid in comprehension and can also serve to direct readers to material of immediate interest and need. Finally, a comprehensive index allows readers to efficiently scan and locate content.

The Contemporary Issues Companion series is an ideal launching point for research on a particular topic. Each anthology in the series is composed of readings taken from an extensive gamut of resources, including periodicals, newspapers, books, government documents, the publications of private and public organizations, and Internet websites. In these volumes, readers will find factual support suitable for use in reports, debates, speeches, and research papers. The anthologies also facilitate further research, featuring a book and periodical bibliography and a list of organizations to contact for additional information.

A perfect resource for both students and the general reader, Greenhaven's Contemporary Issues Companion series is sure to be a valued source of current, readable information on social problems that interest young adults. It is the editors' hope that readers will find the Contemporary Issues Companion series useful as a starting point to formulate their own opinions about and answers to the complex issues of the present day.

Introduction

In January 2003 the outgoing governor of Illinois, George Ryan, commuted the sentences of all of his state's death row inmates. This unprecedented move ignited immediate controversy, eliciting outrage from some quarters, including prosecutors and families of murder victims, and drawing praise from death penalty abolitionists all over the world. Both sides of the debate agreed, however, that it marked a defining moment in the long and complex history of capital punishment in the United States. This was the most damning blow dealt the institution since 1972, when the Supreme Court found that under existing laws the death penalty amounted to "cruel and unusual punishment" and placed a moratorium on its use. Thirty years after that landmark ruling, Ryan's act, which spared the lives of 167 prisoners who had been convicted of murder in the Illinois courts, thrust the issue into the national spotlight once again.

The renewed attention has had profound effects. In the years since Ryan's commutations, the debate about and the use of the death penalty in the United States has undergone dramatic change. In many states, legislation is now being considered to end capital punishment or to put a moratorium on executions. Executions in several states have been halted because of concerns about the use of lethal injection. In 2004 New York's death penalty law was found unconstitutional; in 2005 the Supreme Court struck down laws allowing the execution of juvenile offenders. Death sentences in the country are their lowest in thirty years, executions have sharply declined, and the number of people on death row has decreased. Most Americans still favor the death penalty in principle, but polls show that public support is now evenly divided between the death penalty and life imprisonment as the appropriate punishment for murder.

While Ryan's 2003 decision was a crucial catalyst for these changes, American attitudes toward the death penalty had actually been undergoing quiet revision for a decade before that. In 1994 support for the death penalty was at an all-time high, with 80 percent of Americans favoring its use; by 2003 that percentage had dropped to 67 percent. What accounted for this change? The shift did not come accidentally but was the result of a concerted strategy by anti–death penalty activists to change public opinion on the issue. Troubled by trends in the mid-1990s, abolitionists saw they needed a new tactic if they were to halt the rising rate of executions in the country. They required a new focus and sought to alter the nature of the discussion in order to change the way Americans viewed capital punishment. They downplayed what had traditionally been at the center of the debate—whether it was right or wrong for the state to execute murderers—and emphasized instead the justice of the system currently in place; that is, they shifted the debate from the morality of capital punishment to its fairness as it was actually practiced.

Changing Attitudes Toward the Death Penalty

Since the first execution took place on American soil in 1608, questions about the death penalty have centered on its morality. From the beginning, abolitionists maintained that taking human life under any circumstances was wrong, whereas capital punishment supporters argued that it was justified. In the early days, death penalty opponents looked to the Bible to support their claim, pointing to the Old Testament injunction "Thou shalt not kill." Those favoring the death penalty also used biblical arguments, citing retribution—"an eye for an eye"—as a valid reason for putting murderers to death. When the movement to abolish capital punishment gained ground in the eighteenth century, it was due in large part to Italian philosopher and criminologist Cesare Beccaria's 1767 essay *On*

Crimes and Punishment, which argued that the state could never be justified in taking a human life. Over the next two and a half centuries, public opinion on the issue ebbed and flowed. Even in the space of thirty years, the pendulum swung dramatically—in the mid-1960s a minority of 40 percent of Americans favored capital punishment, and by 1994 that number had doubled.

Both sides also argued over other issues regarding capital punishment, but the morality of the practice was at its core. Death penalty supporters claimed that not only is the state justified in permanently removing a murderer from society, it is obliged to do so to protect its law-abiding citizens from harm. According to supporters, the death penalty is moral not only because it is a fitting punishment but because it prevents further murders: It is a deterrent against crime. Abolitionists historically have denied this assertion. One of the first Americans to argue against deterrence was Dr. Benjamin Rush, the "father of American psychiatry," who in the 1790s claimed that not only is capital punishment not a deterrent but that it has a "brutalization effect," feeding society's appetite for violence and revenge and thus creating more criminal activity.

In the nineteenth century, in response to the writings of European moral philosophers, the abolitionist movement gained strength, and several states did away with the death penalty. Many states enacted discretionary sentencing statutes, which meant that the death penalty was no longer mandated for all capital crimes. In the early decades of the twentieth century, more states sought to outlaw executions. However, after World War I, there was a resurgence in death penalty use, and during the Great Depression more executions took place than at any other time in American history. But this trend began to change once more in the 1950s, perhaps partly in response to the United Nations General Assembly's 1948 Universal Declaration of Human Rights proclaiming a "right to life."

When in the late 1960s opponents began to challenge the legality of the death penalty, the morality of the practice was again of central concern. Activists suggested that the death penalty was "cruel and unusual" punishment and therefore unconstitutional under the Eighth Amendment. They focused on the idea that the United States had an "evolving standard of decency" and that at this historical moment the nation should not tolerate such a form of punishment. In the following decade, opponents emphasized the arbitrariness of sentencing in death penalty cases, claiming that because of this variability the death penalty was "cruel and unusual." It was on these grounds that in *Furman v. Georgia* in 1972 the Supreme Court ruled the death penalty was "wantonly and freakishly imposed" under current states' statutes and declared a moratorium until those laws were rewritten.

A Shift in Focus from Morality to Fairness

The death penalty was reinstated in 1976 after the court ruled that the newly rewritten death penalty statutes in Florida, Georgia, and Texas were constitutional. Although the use of capital punishment resumed and regained support, at this time the debate about the death penalty within the legal and abolitionist communities began to change in important ways. Because of the scrutiny given capital punishment after the *Furman* decision, legal practitioners, scholars, and activists had begun to focus on a number of issues that had emerged regarding its administration. Concentrating on *how* the system of capital punishment in the United States worked, rather than on the morality of the practice in abstract terms, many now concluded that it was fundamentally flawed and therefore in need of overhaul—or better yet, according to abolitionists, elimination.

Among the many flaws in the system that were cited by its opponents was that the death penalty as practiced is deeply racist. Abolitionists cited as evidence the fact that while blacks made up little more than 10 percent of the population, they constitute 40 percent of those on death row. Opponents also argued that capital punishment discriminates against the poor: Although murderers come from all classes, those on death row are almost always at the lowest end of the economic scale. Critics also noted that defendants were often appointed incompetent or disinterested defense counsel.

Increased Public Attention on Capital Punishment

Abolitionists had long held that the death penalty did not work—that it is unfair, costly, and ineffective as a deterrent against crime. But their work now took new form, and received greater notice. Pope John Paul II's visit to the United States in 1993, during which he called for an end to capital punishment, brought the issue national attention. *Dead Man Walking: An Eyewitness Account of the Death Penalty in the United States* by the Catholic nun and activist Sister Helen Prejean won the Pulitzer Prize in 1994 and was made into an Oscar-winning film in 1995. High-profile cases such as that of Karla Faye Tucker, a convicted murderer and former prostitute who seemed to have been rehabilitated while on death row, put a sympathetic face on the issue and made the public rethink imposing the death sentence rather than life imprisonment.

A major turning point for the movement came in 1995, when Rolando Cruz and Alex Hernandez, who were convicted for the 1983 kidnapping and murder of a ten-year-old girl in Chicago and spent ten years on death row, were exonerated and set free. Cruz and Hernandez had been found guilty largely on the false testimony of policy officers and despite the fact that another man had confessed to the crime. The release of the two innocent men drew national attention and built momentum for the abolitionist movement. Activists quickly saw that shining the spotlight on erroneous convictions in death cases captured the public's imagination as no discussion about the morality of capital punishment could. They realized that in order to make progress on this important issue, it would be important to highlight the issue of innocence.

Championing the Cause of Innocence

Spearheaded by Lawrence C. Marshall, who had been Rolando Cruz's lawyer, in 1998 the National Conference on Wrongful Convictions and the Death Penalty was held at Northwestern University School of Law. At the event, twenty-eight innocent former prisoners who had been sentenced to death for crimes they did not commit were brought together on stage. The dramatic visual evidence of a flawed system of justice made national and international news, and the innocence issue was now at the forefront of the debate about capital punishment. The conference organizers made the argument that because of the nature of the system, the only sure way to avoid executing innocent people was to abolish the death penalty

The national discussion on the death penalty had been re-invigorated, and abolitionists found rising support for their work. Just months after the conference came another victory. A group of journalism students at Northwestern began looking into the case of Anthony Porter, a mentally retarded man convicted of a double murder who had been on death row for seventeen years. Working with their professor, David Protess, the students found evidence to completely exonerate Porter just fifty hours before he was scheduled to die in February 1999. The fact that a group of students was the only line of defense for Porter stunned then-governor Ryan. The media took up the issue as well, and reporters at the *Chicago Tribune* began detailing the abuses in the capital punishment system in their series of articles entitled "The Failure of the Death Penalty in Illinois." In 2000 the thirteenth death row inmate in Illinois since 1977 was exonerated, which meant that the number of inmates cleared exceeded the number executed during the same period. Responding to these grim statistics, Ryan declared a moratorium on executions in Illinois, stating, "Until I can be sure, with moral certainty, that no innocent man or woman is facing a lethal injection, no one will meet that fate."

National Reevaluation of the Death Penalty

Ryan's moratorium sent shock waves throughout the country and prompted a nationwide reevaluation of the capital punishment system. President Bill Clinton praised Ryan's move, urging other states to examine their practices; numerous religious groups endorsed a moratorium; and calls for a death penalty freeze were issued at local government levels even in traditionally pro-death penalty constituencies. In June 2000 Professor James Liebman of Columbia University Law School released a comprehensive study reporting that errors had been committed in two-thirds of all capital cases. The report found that the most common errors were incompetent representation by defense attorneys and prosecutorial misconduct.

International pressure was also mounting for the United States to change its position. As the only western industrialized power to retain the use of capital punishment, the United States had for years been urged to change its stance, and international bodies now stepped up their condemnation of the United States policies. Then-secretary general of the United Nations Kofi Annan issued a call for a worldwide moratorium in December 2000 after receiving a petition signed by 3.2 million people seeking an end to capital punishment. In September 2001 the American Bar Association launched the Death Penalty Moratorium Implementation Project as part of its effort to obtain a nationwide moratorium. In a poll that year, more than half of Americans said they supported such a moratorium, while a commission studied whether the death penalty was applied fairly.

The next two years saw a frenzy of moratorium-related activity. The courts heeded the call for greater scrutiny of death cases, and the Supreme Court itself reevaluated the issue. In a particularly significant ruling in the case of *Atkins v. Virginia* in 2002, the Supreme Court made it unconstitutional to execute the mentally retarded. Public opinion on the death penalty system continued to see shifts as well. In the 1990s most American believed that the death penalty was applied fairly, but by the beginning of 2003, this was no longer the case. The views of ordinary Americans began to be reflected in positions taken by politicians and the media, and soon several major U.S. dailies, including the conservative *Chicago Tribune* and *Dallas Morning News*, were calling for an end to capital punishment.

The Uncertain Future of Capital Punishment

When Ryan made his blanket commutations in 2003, the country had already begun a seismic shift in terms of its attitudes about the death penalty. The debate had been moved from the sphere of abstract morality to that of the practical world, and people were paying attention. What Ryan did in 2003, much as he had done in 2000, was to raise awareness of the defects in the system that could not be ignored. Since 2003, because of further scrutiny of the system, Americans have expressed yet deeper doubts. Although polls still show that the death penalty in principle enjoys broad support, in more practical ways it is losing serious ground. Overwhelmingly, juries are favoring life imprisonment over death sentences. In 2006, there were 53 executions in the United States, significantly fewer than the 98 that took place in 1999, and juries sentenced 114 people to die in 2006, less than half the number given the death penalty seven years earlier.

For opponents of the death penalty, these encouraging trends are the fruits of decades of activism. Many death penalty advocates, on the other hand, view the changes that have taken place, both before 2003 and since, with skepticism, seeing many of the statistics delivered by opponents as distorted and overblown. However, other death penalty supporters have been conciliatory and welcomed the scrutiny to the systematic injustices, so that for the first time in history conservatives and liberals have worked together to eliminate the abuses within the capital punishment system. Many supporters of the death penalty argue that the death penalty itself is still an appropriate punishment, but agree that the system needs checks to make sure that justice is truly served. Indeed for some supporters, making the system a reliable one is of supreme importance in order to ensure that the mechanism that would appropriately punish those committing the most heinous crimes against innocent people is not dismantled.

While Americans' views on capital punishment have seen remarkable change in the space of little over a decade, this is certainly not evidence that the death penalty in the United States will be abolished anytime soon. History has shown that opinion on the matter can change swiftly, and the pendulum may yet swing back to increased support for executions. The Supreme Court continues to be divided on the issue, and few politicians have spoken out against it in principle. However, what the current climate does indicate is that the abolitionists' strategy has worked. What is of most importance to Americans today is not the rightness or wrongness of capital punishment but discovering and putting an end to the problems that have caused the system to fail. In this new phase of the capital punishment debate, Americans have little interest in rhetoric or abstract arguments about the morality of the death penalty; instead, they are looking for assurances that their system of justice works.

CHAPTER 1

The Death Penalty in the United States

Reevaluating the Death Penalty

Hugo Adam Bedau

Hugo Adam Bedau is a professor of philosophy at Tufts University and one of the most outspoken opponents of the death penalty in the United States. In the following article, he surveys the current trends in the United States that indicate widespread support for the death penalty. Despite this evidence, he says, numerous other factors—including public preference for long-term imprisonment, the ineffectiveness of capital punishment as a deterrent, the flawed and racist legal system, questions about the unconstitutionality of the administration of the death penalty, and the execution of innocent persons—show that the institution is undergoing a major revaluation that, he hopes, will lead to its abolition in the near future.

In the new millennium, the death penalty continues to hold the United States in its grip and it is impossible to predict how soon that grip will weaken, much less disappear altogether. Let us begin by looking at some of the major factors supporting the current status of the death penalty:

- The Supreme Court's ruling in 1976 that the death penalty as such does not violate the Constitution remains intact. Circumstances under which the current members of the Supreme Court would decide to reverse the decisions of a generation ago are difficult to imagine.

- The *de jure* moratorium on executions from 1968 to 1976 spared the lives of hundreds of death row prisoners, but it led to few lasting improvements in the statu-

Hugo Adam Bedau, *The Death Penalty Beyond Abolition*. Strasbourg, Council of Europe Publishing, 2004. Copyright © Council of Europe 2004. Reproduced by permission.

tory or constitutional protections of due process of law and equal protection of the law in death penalty cases; and did little to create an informed body of public opinion against this form of punishment.

- The annual number of executions has grown remarkably in recent years: from 1 in 1981, 18 in 1986, 14 in 1991, 45 in 1996, to 85 in 2000—the most since 1951. There is no evident reason to expect this number to decline or even hold steady in the near future. Correspondingly, the number of prisoners on death row (more than 3,700 in the spring of 2003) has never been greater.

- Today, appellate review by the federal courts of state court convictions and sentences in capital cases is fraught with impediments, thanks to congressional efforts and Supreme Court rulings aimed at bringing finality (at the cost of fairness) to appellate litigation in capital cases.

- No member of the current Supreme Court is on record opposed to the death penalty on the ground that it violates the 8th amendment prohibition of "cruel and unusual punishment"—or on any other constitutional ground.

- No state legislature in recent years has abolished the death penalty.

- No state supreme court in recent years has judged the death penalty to be inconsistent with the state's own constitution.

- No state chief executive in recent years, with one major exception, has commuted the sentences of his state's death row prisoners on the ground that the death penalty is in violation of human rights—or, for that matter, on any other ground. The exception is former Governor George Ryan of Illinois, who early in 2003 extended clemency to all 171 of the state's death row prisoners.

- No established public voice has caught and held the nation's attention as a critic of the death penalty; both presidential candidates in the recent general election (2000) supported capital punishment.

- The nation's politics continue to be distorted and corrupted by the stranglehold the death penalty has on elective and appointive officials. The worry is widespread that the surest way to end one's political career is to become known as an opponent of the death penalty.

- Juveniles (persons under eighteen years of age) are still liable to be sentenced to death and executed in some states.

- In the mid-1990s, Congress enacted new federal death penalty statutes, including a few involving no homicide. These laws also empowered the federal government to pre-empt state jurisdiction, thus enabling the prosecution of a crime as a death penalty case in states (such as Michigan and Massachusetts, among others) that have abolished this penalty.

- Federal judges appointed by the current Republican administration are not likely to find many reasons to rule against convictions and death sentences in the capital cases that come before them for review.

- The effort to obtain a nationwide moratorium on executions, to provide an opportunity for careful study of the administration of the death penalty, is stalled (as of early 2003) both in Congress and in more than a dozen states, where such measures have been proposed.

- Public opinion polls continue to show majority support for the death penalty for murder.

- Early in 2001, the execution of [Oklahoma City bomber] Timothy McVeigh was the first under federal law in thirty-seven years and was carried out by the recently elected Republican administration of President George W. Bush, known for his support of the death penalty during his tenure as Governor of Texas, during which he presided over more executions than any other governor this century. For the first time in decades, the nation witnessed an execution that dramatically publicised support for the death penalty in the executive branch of the federal government.

Arrayed against these facts are a variety of considerations that encourage a somewhat more optimistic view for those who favour abolition.

Public Opinion

Common knowledge has it that a large majority of the American public supports the death penalty (as noted above). But the truth is more complex. First survey research shows that a majority (63%) of the public currently accepts the death penalty; this is the lowest public support in twenty years. Second, the same research shows that the public is evenly split (46% to 45%) in its preference for the death penalty over long-term imprisonment. For reasons not entirely clear, this sharp contrast between what the public professes to accept and what it professes to prefer has not been effectively communicated to politicians, whose chief reason for opposing abolition is the belief that the electorate demands it.

Elusive Support

For various reasons peculiar to American history, the death penalty today is largely a relic of the system of racial injustice and anti-black violence that runs like a bloody wound through the nation's social fabric. The death penalty system is manifestly strongest in the old Confederacy (virtually co-extensive with the so-called Bible Belt) in the deep South. There is little visible support for this form of punishment in the nation's major metropolitan newspapers or among academic social scientists. Political commentators have been divided on the issue, but for reasons to be mentioned below are increasingly vocal in expressing doubts about the system. Whereas the law journals and book store shelves overflow with every kind of criticism of the death penalty and its flaws, there are no recent books and few articles arguing the case for capital punishment. Opponents of the death penalty have long ago won the battle of words—and of research, too.

The Capital Jury Project

Most research against the death penalty in the United States during the previous century focused on one or the other of two main topics: deterrence and racism. Social scientists argued persuasively that there was no convincing evidence of the superior preventive efficacy of executions. They argued even more persuasively that the death penalty system as it actually operates, especially in the South, reflected the historic racism of the larger society. This research, conducted in the 1980s, established the race-of-victim factor: persons convicted of killing a white victim were 4.3 times more likely to be sentenced to death than those convicted of killing a non-white victim.

A wholly new line of research was inaugurated in 1990 with the creation of the Capital Jury Project. Underway in fourteen states, the aim of the project is to study how capital jurors make their life or death sentencing decisions. Based on in-depth interviews with a thousand former capital jurors, the chief question to be answered is whether capital trial juries conform to or violate the standards laid down by the Supreme

Court in a series of decisions since 1976. Results to date suggest that jurors typically do not fully understand the instructions from the trial judge, and that even when they do, they do not comply with them. For example, four out of ten jurors indicated that they believed they were *required* to vote for death sentence if they found the murder was "heinous, vile, or depraved". But the law states that such a finding is only one of several sufficient conditions of a death sentence and did not by itself (as these jurors believed) make a death sentence mandatory.

This research is significant for at least two reasons. First, it forces one to conclude that the "guided discretion" in death penalty sentencing endorsed by the Supreme Court in 1976 has not worked out in practice as intended. Second, it bolsters criticism of the system based on the actual experience of former capital trial jurors who have given first-hand testimony about how they discharged their awesome responsibility in deciding between a punishment of life in prison or death.

Supreme Court Justices Express Their Doubts

The Supreme Court has not (as of this writing) ruled in favour of the constitutionality of any of the non-homicidal state and federal death penalty statutes. Instead, since 1976 the Supreme Court has without exception ruled unconstitutional such non-homicidal statutes, and it is by no means certain that it will soon alter its path in a new direction. Since 1976 several members of the Supreme Court—most recently justice Harry A. Blackmun (1908–99) and Justice Lewis F. Powell (1907–98)— have concluded that the death penalty as administered in the United States is an unconstitutional violation of due process of law, equal protection of law, and is a cruel and unusual punishment however administered.

In the summer of 2001, Justice Sandra Day O'Connor, not an opponent of the death penalty as such, voiced her concerns about the capacity of the nation's courts to administer a fair and effective system of capital punishment. She even went so far as to say that the current system "may well be allowing some innocent defendants to be executed. Doubts of this sort have proved in the past to be the preface to a refusal altogether (in Justice Blackmun's words) to tinker any further with" the machinery of death.

Miscarriages of Justice

By far the most influential and troubling aspect of the death penalty in the United States today is the demonstrable failure of the system to convict and sentence only the guilty. Incontrovertible evidence of innocent men being wrongfully convicted and saved from execution only by the diligent efforts of persons outside the system, such as journalism students, family members, newspaper reporters, dramatically points up the problem. No one can seriously believe that all such errors have been detected in time to avert the execution of someone actually innocent. At the conclusion of a recent federal death penalty case in Massachusetts, the trial judge Michael A. Ponsor observed:

> [A] legal regime relying on the death penalty will inevitably execute innocent people. . . . Mistakes will be made. . . .

The extensive publicity given to many such cases, especially in Illinois, prompted Governor George Ryan to institute a moratorium on all executions in the state pending review and remedy of the procedures and practices involved in capital cases. Of the many factors that can weaken national support for the death penalty, this is unquestionably the most influential.

Maladministration of the Death Penalty

Lawyers familiar with the way the death penalty system actually works at present in the United States have amply documented the outrageous practices, unfair rulings, the abuse of discretion, tolerance of injustice in many forms—above all, the problems arising from poverty and race—that occur far too often and are typical of the system at its worst. Recent research at Columbia University Law School has shown that between 1973 and 1995, "[appellate] courts found serious, reversible error in nearly 7 out of 10 of the thousands of capital sentences [investigated]." After state appellate courts threw out 47% of the death sentences they reviewed, due to grave flaws, subsequent federal appellate review found "serious error undermining the reliability of the outcome in 40% of the remaining sentence."

One important step toward mitigating these failures would be the Innocence Protection Act, a bill filed in Congress early in 2001 with bi-partisan support. If enacted, the bill would institute a wide variety of procedural changes affecting the administration of the federal death penalty. While not advancing the cause of abolition directly, this piece of legislation (like the moratorium) would make prominent and enduring the concern over fairness in the death penalty system. If, as most abolitionists believe, it is functionally impossible to have a fair death penalty system, that lesson would effectively be taught by the efforts to comply with the requirements of the act.

Incompetence and Unavailability of Defense Counsel

Standards for counsel representing a capital defendant vary from state to state and are often remarkably low. The Supreme Court ruled in 1984 that a plea for retrial based on a claim of ineffective assistance of trial counsel would not succeed unless it were shown that counsel failed to provide "reasonably effective assistance" and that but for counsel's errors a different outcome was probable. In 1996, Congress ended federal funding for post-conviction defender organisations, leaving appellate litigation in capital cases to be financed entirely by the states, with enormously varied results. In 2000, the Supreme

Court ruled that counsel who slept on and off during trial could be said to have provided inadequate representation only if the defendant could show that his counsel while dozing had missed important aspects of the trial proceedings. Since a convicted defendant's successful appeal depends on the skill and devotion of his counsel, it is deeply troubling to learn from a report in *The New York Times* that in the summer of 2001,

> ... [d]ozens of inmates on death row lack lawyers for their appeals, in part because private law firms are increasingly unwilling to take on burdensome, expensive and emotionally wrenching capital cases...

Moratorium

Beginning in 1987 the American Bar Association (ABA) has advocated a variety of proposals designed to provide better protection for capital defendants, but without much evident effect. In 1997, however, the ABA's House of Delegates recommended a nationwide moratorium on the death penalty, to enable a thorough review of the administration of capital punishment with an eye to revisions in longstanding practices that would reduce, if not eliminate, the risk of erroneous convictions, sentences, and executions.

In the 1980s, there was little interest outside confirmed abolitionist circles for such a death penalty moratorium; in 2001 the subject has been widely debated and in several cases nearly enacted by popular demand. The great merit of the moratorium movement is that it promises heightened scrutiny of the workings of the system by persons not hitherto deeply concerned with it one way or the other. It also empowers informed abolitionists to persuade fence-sitters that the longstanding complaints registered against the system are not exaggerated and they are not isolated and infrequent occurrences.

Muted Political Support

While it remains true that the presidential candidates in 2000 supported the death penalty, they did it in a relatively muted manner. The chief effect was largely to remove the death penalty from the campaign—probably a good thing, since the typical modern political campaign has never been a helpful forum for debate and public education on this issue. Whereas in the general election of 1988, Republicans loudly criticised the Democratic presidential candidate for his opposition to the death penalty, Republican strategists in 2000 made no effort to boast of their candidate's conspicuous support for the death penalty. Sensing that the public would not respond favourably to portraying Governor George W. Bush as "tough on crime", proved by the record number of death sentences carried out during his term of office (152), Republicans let the death penalty become virtually a non-issue.

The Irrationality of Death Penalty Support

During the previous century professed support for the death penalty rested chiefly on belief in its superior preventive powers: it would deter crimes that no less severe punishment would, and it would prevent crimes through incapacitation in a manner superior to imprisonment. Or so death penalty supporters alleged. In any case, if the death penalty were to be used for various crimes and not only murder (as indeed was the case until the 1970s), its defence would have to rest mainly on its preventive (deterrent and incapacitative) powers. But by the end of the century, with the death penalty confined to homicidal crimes, the deterrence argument had largely been abandoned, owing in part to the lack of convincing empirical support. (In early 2000, only 8% of those who supported the death penalty did so on the ground that they believed it to be a deterrent and "sets an example." Four years earlier, the nation's leading professional criminologists announced their conclusion that the death penalty was not a superior deterrent to long prison sentences.)

Instead of prevention, retributive considerations are the chief support on which defenders of the death penalty now rely: murderers deserve to die. (As the then governor of Florida put it in 1989, "I believe in the death penalty for one who has taken someone else's life.") From an empirical point of view, this proposition is difficult to argue for or against—except to note that unalloyed retributivism is not so widely shared as some would believe. If trial courts, prosecutors, governors, and legislatures believed it, they would favour mandatory death penalties, they would oppose plea bargaining (avoiding a death sentence by confessing to the crime, or by giving testimony against one's co-defendants), and they would oppose clemency except where the defendant could prove he was innocent. In actual practice, nothing of the sort happens. The Supreme Court has ruled against every form of mandatory death penalty it has reviewed, prosecutors would be unable to do their job if they abandoned plea bargaining, and trial courts bring in a death sentence in only a fraction of the cases where in theory it would be appropriate. The rarity of commutations is the sole remaining stronghold of retributive considerations. In short, retribution in the form of "a life for a life" is daily subordinated to other considerations by those who nominally support the death penalty and have the responsibility to administer it. This is very unlikely to change in the near future, and these compromises with retribution point up the frailty of any rational foundation on which to rest support for the death penalty. . . .

"Closure" or Reconciliation?

The point of an execution, we are often now told, is "closure", which is understood to mean relief from the suffering endured by the surviving family members, a relief they believe they can find only in knowing their loved one's murderer is dead, or—better yet, in actually witnessing his death. On this view, the preventive powers of the death penalty as well as the moral claims made on behalf of retribution are subordinated to its alleged emotional and psychological benefits. In recent years in the United States the annual criminal homicide rate of around 15,000–18,000 deaths yields some 100,000 immediate family members who are potential seekers of closure.

What they find, often enough, however, is something quite different. Sister Helen Prejean, author of *Dead Man Walking* (1993), has served as a spiritual counsellor to many families of prisoners on death row and has also been confronted by closure seekers. As they witness the trial and appeals and perhaps testify at the sentencing phase of the trial, she has noted that "they learn new details of the crime, and with each new turn of the trial and its aftermath the media call them to get a reaction." This is hardly a recipe for "closure," since it feeds the anger and keeps alive the resentment so many survivors have toward the murderer.

Taking a completely different approach is Murder Victims Families for Reconciliation (MVFR), founded in 1976. A growing national organisation, it has impeccable credentials: Its members, too, know what it is like to survive the murder of a loved one. They believe that nursing their anger and hatred serves no good purpose—indeed, the very opposite. MFVR has brought its message of reconciliation to many legislative hearings, media events, and execution vigils across the nation. Many other abolitionist organisations are active in the United States today (the National Coalition to Abolish the Death Penalty, also founded in 1976, has sixty state affiliates and has sixty other regional and national organisations affiliated with it). MVFR, with its uniquely brave and impressive message, may well be the most persuasive and exemplary in the years ahead.

International Human Rights Law

Bit by bit, opposition to the death penalty on the ground that it violates the human rights of the prisoner is making headway in the United States. Despite the refusal of the federal government to sign or ratify the Second Optional Protocol to the International Covenant on Civil and Political Rights, aiming at the abolition of the death penalty, or even to ratify the covenant without reservations, these and other provisions of international human rights law have increasingly become part of the debate in the United States over the death penalty. This influence was evident in the Supreme Court's decision in 2002 forbidding the execution of anyone who was mentally retarded.

Execution of the mentally ill, execution of persons who committed a capital crime under the age of 18, and enactment of new capital crimes—each of these is still done in various US jurisdictions, each violates international human rights law, and each has come under increasing criticism. More argument and agitation on this ground can safely be predicted. They are bound to have an impact, however indirect, on the complacency with which the death penalty is accepted.

Conclusion

In the summer of 1972, when the Supreme Court ruled that the then prevailing administration of the death penalty was "cruel and unusual punishment," several experienced observers of the death penalty scene in the United States (including this writer) believed that a major and irreversible step toward total abolition had been taken, and they predicted that there would be no more executions in the nation. In the nearly three decades since then, forty states and the federal government have re-enacted death penalty statutes and sentenced more than 6,000 convicted murderers to death; two dozen of these jurisdictions have carried out more than 700 death sentences. So much for ill-advised predictions.

At present, the death penalty in the United States is undergoing the most extensive criticism and re-evaluation in its history. This attention is bound to lead to dissatisfaction and a change of mind in many of its current supporters, especially those who want a death penalty but want fairness in the way it is administered as well. How that growing discontent can be channelled into effective political opposition to the death penalty remains to be seen. There are no unambiguous signs that this is taking place or is about to take place. With the passage of time, the irony of the present situation—the United States often boasts of its concern over human rights violations elsewhere in the world (and rightly so), yet the courts, the legislatures, and the people fail to see such violations where our practice of the death penalty is concerned—is bound to be sobering. One can only hope that awareness of this fact and a willingness to act on it to rid the nation of the death penalty will come sooner rather than later.

The Navajo Opt Out of the Death Penalty

Marilyn Berlin Snell

Marilyn Berlin Snell is a writer whose work has appeared in the New York Times, Sierra Magazine, Mother Jones, *the* Los Angeles Times, *and many other publications. In the following essay, she recounts the story of Wallace Dale, whose daughter, Deirdre, was brutally murdered near her home on the Navajo Reservation in New Mexico. Murder on the reservation, Snell explains, is not unusual; it goes hand in hand with the extreme poverty and violent crime that are part of daily life there. But traditional Navajo beliefs do not condone the death penalty, and the Navajo Nation has deferred to the principles that human life should never be taken in vengeance and that justice should focus on healing and bringing life into balance. Snell discusses how in the face of a new set of social problems the Navajo people are reconsidering their beliefs and reformulating their tribal justice system. She shows too how Dale's personal experience made him question his people's position and consider whether the death penalty is about revenge or justice.*

Deirdre Dale, who according to her father looked more like a china doll than a Navajo, was on her way to a pay phone near her family's trailer in Gallup, New Mexico, when she hitched a ride from two men and a woman in a baby blue Buick LeSabre. The men had been drinking and their first stop once the girl was in the car was to get more liquor. While the men were gone, the woman—a grade-school teacher—accused 16-year-old Deirdre of flirting. Hearing the two screaming, the men dove back into the car and began pursuing Deirdre. She fought back, and things escalated.

When Deirdre didn't come home, her parents filed a police report. Then they sought the help of a medicine woman, who spread the deep-red dirt of the reservation on the floor, had a vision and wrote part of it in the soil. She could see all of what had happened to Deirdre but didn't want to tell. When Deirdre's father, Wallace Dale, demanded answers, she told him that his daughter would show up in a few days.

The teen's body was found, strangled and burned, in a ravine seven days later; nearby were a beer can, a white sock, and a clump of hair caught on some weeds. The Gallup medical examiner's office tagged the body "Jane Begay," a common surname among the Diné, or The People, as they call themselves.

Wallace Dale tells the story of his daughter's death in clipped, even sentences; the only time his eyes mist over is when he talks about how the anniversaries of her birth and death still get to him. And the only time he laughs is when he reminisces about growing up traditional in the remote folds of the reservation's Chuska Mountains. His mother hewed to Navajo dress and the ancient creation stories; his father, a Comanche, practiced the healing arts of medicine men. The family raised sheep and horses, and grew corn, squash, and beans. There was no running water, electricity, or gas. "It was a lot of work but fun, and we learned a lot from it too," Dale says. "I always held on to their ways. Without them, we all would have been lost."

But after Deirdre was murdered, tradition could not keep Dale anchored. He got sick; bills piled up; his marriage fell apart. He was consumed by fantasies of revenge, and he came to believe that his people's tradition was getting in the way of justice for Deirdre. It was time, he decided, for the Navajo to embrace the death penalty.

Violence as a Sickness

There's something timeless and isolated, something that outsiders often find romantic, about the Navajo reservation, where roughly 168,000 tribal members live in a space the size of West Virginia. Grandmothers visit the trading posts in velvet shirts and long skirts, scarves fastened beneath their chins against the desert sun. Though pickup trucks are ubiquitous, many families still walk their sheep to summer and winter camps, through sandstone slot canyons and unnamed valleys dotted with sagebrush. The Nation's official seal features 48 outward-pointing arrowheads in an unbroken circle, symbolizing the Navajos' unique relationship with the United States: Never broken up, never truly defeated, the tribe has clung to its sovereignty, its culture, and its harsh, beloved homeland.

None of that, however, has insulated the Navajo from cataclysmic levels of violence. The violent crime rate on the reservation, where 60 percent of the population is under 25, is sharply higher than the national average; alcohol, drugs, poverty, and a creeping shift from traditional clan culture to gang culture have fueled an epidemic of lethal beatings, stabbings, and execution-style shootings. It is hard to find anyone on the reservation who has not had a family member murdered. Yet whenever federal prosecutors have considered seeking the death penalty in a murder case on the reservation, the Navajo have objected. The Nation's "cultural beliefs and traditions value life in all forms and instruct against the taking of human life for vengeance," Herb Yazzie, the tribe's former attorney general (and now the chief justice of its Supreme Court), wrote to the U.S. attorney in New Mexico in 1998. Navajo custom views violence as a sickness that must be treated rather than as an evil that must be destroyed; the Navajo, for obvious historical reasons, also fear ceding to outsiders the right to decide their fate.

This conflict came into sharper relief with the 1994 federal crime bill, in which Congress expanded the death penalty but also included a clause allowing tribes to choose whether to "opt in." Ever since, tribes across the country have periodically been convulsed by the opt-in debate. But perhaps no tribe—

and no other community in America—has wrestled with the question as often, as wrenchingly, and through as remarkable a process as the Navajo.

Healing with Words

Though used in small doses, words are considered powerful medicine in Navajo creation stories: The maternal grandfather of all the deities is the Talking God, whose purview includes the passing on of custom and tradition. Enormous distances between neighbors—there is only one person here for every 89 acres—and an individualistic streak have tended to keep Navajo family clans separated; disputes were traditionally worked out via gatherings where issues were talked through in public. It's a distinct form of problem-solving in keeping with Navajo morality, which emphasizes above all a return to social balance.

It was this custom that the tribal government's Public Safety Committee drew on when, in late 2003, it announced a series of public forums to examine whether the Nation should change its stance on the death penalty. Two years had gone by since Deirdre Dale's death as well as the murder of a nine-year-old girl and her grandmother, killed and dismembered by two men who wanted their truck. Federal prosecutors were seeking the death penalty in that case, something they had not done with Deirdre's killers, one of whom had been able to plead out to a 12-year sentence. (The other man got life without parole; the woman, four and a half years.)

Wallace Dale was one of the first people to speak when the talks began in the New Mexico outpost of Shiprock, a dusty town along the San Juan River named for the volcanic monolith that rises nearly 2,000 feet from the desert floor like a Navajo sky-scraper "My daughter Deirdre L. Dale was murdered on February 24, 2001," he told the Public Safety Committee in Shiprock's chapter house. When the crime is heinous, he said, execution "is not revenge." Photos of the meeting show Dale, holding up a picture of Deirdre, his face drawn and pale. He looks close to tears.

Navajo Justice

Kathleen Bowman, the director of the tribe's Public Defender's Office, understood Dale's torment. In her youth, she had been on the fence about the death penalty. Her grandfather had been robbed and beaten to death in Gallup; a nephew had been stabbed to death the night before his 23rd birthday; a cousin had been murdered in Phoenix. Two weeks before she was to take the Arizona bar exam in 1986, Bowman learned that her older brother had been killed by a drunk driver—her stepfather's nephew. "When my children told me, I screamed and cried, and it echoed through the law school," she says.

The next day, the boy who had killed her brother came to her mother's house, where everyone had gathered to mourn. "My sisters were angry," she recalls. "They didn't want to speak to him. They wanted him gone." At that point, something shifted for her. "I told my sisters, 'You can't think like that. It could easily have been one of our own brothers driving. It could happen to anybody, so you need to treat this person like a human.' That's when I realized that it's not about punishment."

Barely over 5 feet tall, with long, dark brown hair that she curls at the ends, Bowman tends toward self-deprecation. Her office defends Navajos, most of them young, many of them accused of vicious crimes. In giving me directions to her office in Window Rock, she offered no street address but told me to "head toward the rock" for which the town is named.

There were rocks everywhere—huge, rosy slabs and boulders to the east, north, and south, but I saw none with a hole in it. It wasn't until locals pointed me in the right direction that I noticed the massive gap in the sandstone. To find Bowman's office, I'd had to orient myself to the land and the four directions, something I found difficult in this otherworldly place. In trying to navigate among the Navajo—a people who are given to long silences during conversation, with a language so impenetrable it was used as code during World War II—it is easy to get lost.

"There are things that go on here that are pretty scary" Bowman says. "But I don't look at the defendants as evil." Some are "psychopaths, sociopaths, that we will never be able to help," but most of the crimes she sees are bound up with a near-desperate degree of drinking or drug use. "People are medicating themselves; it's almost like a hopelessness."

Bowman told me about a famous 19th-century legal case. In 1881, a Lakota Sioux named Spotted Tail was killed by another Lakota, Crow Dog. A tribal council was called, the families of the two men gathered, and it was agreed that in order to restore harmony to the tribe, Crow Dog and his family would pay the deceased's kin $600, eight horses, and one blanket. The U.S. territorial court threw out this judgment, put Crow Dog on trial, and sentenced him to death by hanging. The case made it to the U.S. Supreme Court, which decreed that tribes were entitled to adjudicate crimes among their own as they saw fit. Congress then stepped in to strip tribes of that right, and today's tribal courts are restricted to dispensing fines and no more than a year of jail time, with major crimes mostly dealt with in federal court.

In Bowman's view, punitive justice is eroding the very traditions that are also the community's best hope for battling the epidemic of brutality. Navajo justice, she says, focuses on the concept of *nályééb*, or making society whole again; it has little use for punishment for its own sake. Several years ago, Bowman had a client who had stabbed his friend while both were drinking. "We were in tribal court, and I proposed an agreement that my client would pay restitution to the man he stabbed in the amount of $1,000—an amount that my client would definitely feel. My client had to make amends for his conduct, and the other person received restitution for his injury." The families agreed, and the charges were dropped, No one went to prison.

Opting Out of the Death Penalty

I met Delores Dale, Deirdre's mother and Wallace's ex-wife, at her trailer outside Gallup. Blue plastic butterfly clips held her black hair back from her eyes, which never met mine. We leaned against my car, looking down the dusty, rutted street Deirdre had walked on her way to the pay phone.

The pain that began when Deirdre went missing continued to burn through the family for years. Deirdre's older sister was racked by guilt: Before walking off that day, Deirdre had asked her for a ride to the pay phone, but she'd refused. Her brother, Doran, took to drinking and pot-smoking, became depressed, and was hospitalized off and on. At 4 A.M. the night before we met, Delores had learned that Doran was in the hospital again, his jaw shattered by fists and boots in an alcohol-fueled rampage. "He's in a bad way" she said. "He's still angry and sad. Makes me sad to see him like that."

A while back, Delores asked a medicine man to do traditional healing ceremonies for her son: the Blessing Way, which invokes the holy people to come around and bestow favorable conditions, and the Evil Way, whose chants are used for curing sickness caused by ghosts. It helped, she said, but what they also needed was grief counseling, and there were no such services nearby. Part of the problem was Navajo tradition's taboo against talking about death, she said: "It happens, the funeral is done, and they don't bring it up again." Delores had gone to the public hearings to say that custom, in this case, was doing more harm than good. "They don't want to talk about death," she said, "but our generation is different. You have to talk about it"

When the Public Safety Committee finally released its report on the hearings last year, it did urge more help for victims' families. It also recommended that the Nation continue to opt out of the death penalty. The hearings had not fully settled the matter; like Sisyphus' stone, the death penalty debate would someday be set tumbling again.

For Wallace Dale, though, the hearings did bring a kind of resolution. At the last of the talks, he rose to deliver what seemed to be his familiar exhortation: He still couldn't eat or sleep; he had $9,000 in medical bills; people who had lost a loved one to violence needed counseling. "It can ruin your life" he said. And then he said that he no longer wanted his daughter's killers put to death. "I'm changing my views," he explained simply, "because of the comments and opinions of the people."

"It took me a while," Dale says now. "I had to do a lot of thinking." He had crisscrossed the reservation to attend the hearings, and all those miles traveled, all the words spoken and heard, had changed him. He showed me a paper he wrote for his English 101 class at Southwestern Indian Polytechnic Institute, where he is studying electronics. "Our elders, our medicine men and medicine women, teach us that life is sacred, life is precious, life is holy," it read. "They teach us to pray for all people, all living creatures both great and small, and to have respect for our mother earth so that in return she will give us a good blessing. When a murder occurs, it is through prayers, compassion, love, respect, and dignity that harmony is brought back into our lives so that we may be whole again."

Last year, at age 44, Dale made the president's list at the polytechnic institute and was chosen an "Outstanding Student of the Year." He says the death penalty talks helped him heal; so did grief counseling in Albuquerque, and the Native American Church on the reservation. With the hint of a smile, he offers a term he picked up at school: "It's called 'eclectic learning.' Navajos learned silversmithing from the Mexicans; they learned to make pottery from the Pueblo. They take what's useful and it becomes theirs."

Some time ago, Dale went to see a medicine man who told him that Deirdre was in another world, a spirit world not far from this one, and that she had a job to do. When Dale cried, she worried about him, and that was holding her back. "I really thought about that, and I let her go," he says. "It seemed like a lot of weight was lifted off my shoulder."

The United States Needs to Exercise Retribution in Considering the Death Penalty

Robert Blecker

Robert Blecker, a professor at New York Law School, is a nationally known retribution advocate of the death penalty. In the following article, he points out how in the last thirty years legal attitudes to the death penalty laws have undergone dizzying change and how society has become increasingly split on how to punish capital crimes. Blecker suggests we can better understand this complex contemporary problem by looking back to the ancient Greeks and seeing how their system of law responded to different types of killings. Blecker points out the problems with the modern legal system, which attempts to provide impartiality, distance, fairness, and consistency when imposing sentences for capital murder cases. Emotion, he says, should in fact play an important role in sentencing for individual cases. Like the ancient Greeks, Blecker calls for a "transcendent" concept of justice that blends consistency with a defendant's particular circumstances and recognizes that each killer and each killing is unique and must be responded to accordingly.

Abolitionists attack capital punishment as cruel. Its administration, they insist, is inconsistent, and the jurisprudence which supports it is incoherent. Furthermore, they claim, death as punishment is disproportionate to any crime and out of step with essential values which are at the core of a mature Western democracy. Their attack is substantive (the law cannot adequately define who deserves to die) and procedural (the process of deciding who lives or dies must, but

Robert Blecker, "Ancient Greece's Death Penalty Dilemma and Its Influence on Modern Society," *USA Today*, July 2006, pp. 60–65. Copyright © 2006 Society for the Advancement of Education. Reproduced by permission.

cannot, simultaneously embrace the two core constitutional values of fairness and consistency). Every individual defendant must be treated as a unique human being and, at the same time, like cases must be treated alike.

Death penalty advocates also look to human dignity as their touchstone. They agree that, unless the practice is worthy of a humane culture and the procedures consistent with basic long-standing core commitments, it must be abolished. These last 30 years during the death penalty's "modern era," in a society deeply split over how to punish murder, and with a Supreme Court regulating every aspect, the changes to death penalty jurisprudence appear to be fast and furious. Taking the long view, however, homicide and how to react to it remain the most conservative aspects of law in Western culture. Thus, we can better hope to resolve this contemporary and complex problem by stepping back 2,500 years, drawing from our cultural wellspring in ancient Greece where Western genius first flowered.

"Blood Price"—Punishment for Homicide in Ancient Greece

Human beings feel a primal urge to retaliate. From 1200–800 B.C., homicide strictly was personal. If the killer did not escape, the victim's family caught and killed him, or they accepted a "blood price," settling it monetarily—buying the killer peace and the victim's survivors some measure of satisfaction. Yet, within a few centuries after the musings of the [early Greek] poet Homer, a great change took place: The community became consciously and emotionally involved.

The decisive change was the idea (a feeling, actually) that "blood pollutes the land." Thus, independently and at about the same time that the ancient Hebrews in their Bible rejected the "blood price," refusing to allow the killer to buy his way out, so, too, did the ancient Greeks. Repulsed by blood pollution and rejecting the blood price, they expressed the ultimate value of human life concretely—the convicted murderer must die.

In Athens, once the victim's family publicly accused him, the defendant was considered polluting. Anybody who saw him in a public place was allowed to kill him on the spot. The victim's family still might prefer a monetary settlement, but the response to homicide became more than personal payback. Only punishment that canceled the pollution would end the public threat, and only the community could determine how much punishment was enough. This feeling that the victim's blood morally pollutes us until the killer is dealt with adequately—a deep-seated retributive urge—is what moves death penalty advocates today.

Different Punishments for Different Types of Killings

While Homer's epics reveal no distinctions among homicides, except a special horror at killing one's own kin, within a few centuries the Athenians established disparate courts to try separate types of killings. The Aeropagus, the highest court of legal guardians, sat en masse to try premeditated murderers and would-be tyrants. A lesser court of 51 members tried unpremeditated killings: another dealt with justifiable killings. . . .

Finally, there was a special denunciatory court for unidentified killers, animals, or inanimate objects that had caused the death of human beings. If this seems primitive, consider the intense public concern when [in 2005] a California jury condemned Scott Peterson to die, although it is unlikely the state ever will execute him for the murder of his wife Laci and their unborn child. In this case, supporters of the death penalty focused on the jury's declaration of death, its official denunciation, as significant in and of itself. This basic impulse to mark off officially and denounce the worst killings long runs through Western culture.

In ancient Athens, at any time before trial, the accused voluntarily could go into exile, thereby confessing his guilt. Banished forever, still contaminated and contaminating, he never could return. The ancients put it out of their own power to reconsider. No matter how old and infirm the killer, how distant the memory of the victim, how diminished the cost to the family, the pollution never ended—"the voice of your brother's blood" cried out forever. . . .

With the idea of "blood pollution" in the Old Testament and ancient Greece, humanity had taken a giant step. Blood pollution binds the community to the slain. In "the best governed State," declared Solon, the great law-giver, "those who were not wronged were no less diligent in prosecuting wrongdoers than those who had personally suffered," and not merely from abstract duty. "Citizens, like members of the same body, should feel and resent one another's injuries." Ancient utilitarians must have urged execution to prevent a bad harvest, the surest proof of contamination. However, blood pollution—the voice of the dead crying out in anger and anguish as his killer, living free, pollutes the land—calls to us in a manner not strictly empirical, moves us to act from motives not strictly rational. Nevertheless, to those who feel morally obliged, this urge to punish is real.

The Constitutionality of Death

Constitutional contests over the death penalty during the modern era sometimes have focused on substance—finding or fashioning objective categories that can make a killer deserve to die. These "aggravators" often include the nature of the victims (children, police officers, multiple victims) or the motive of the killer (for money; sadistically, for kicks) or the methods of killing (torture, mutilation). Other substantive limits categorically exclude entire classes of killers from the "worst of the worst." These include the mentally retarded and juveniles, for instance. Mostly, however, the contest has focused on process. Not so much who deserves to die, but how to establish it.

Long before the philosopher Plato came along, the debate was joined. "You cannot step in the same river twice," Heraclitus, the dark philosopher of Ephesus, famously summed up, "for fresh waters flow on." Today's Heracliteans deny that we can categorize homicides meaningfully in advance by relying on real differences among types of killings or killers. Everything is in flux: no two situations ever repeat. Each killing and killer is unique. General roles never can deal adequately with nonrepeating concrete specific situations. Those in power arbitrarily and capriciously execute whom they choose and then call it justice, today's moral anarchists insist. Thus, for them, as for Heraclitus, everything is relative: opposites are identical. One person's "martyr" is another's "mass murderer." The difference between the worst of the worst and the thoroughly justified is ad hoc, depending on who had the power to make the label stick.

A couple of centuries after Heraclitus, Socrates squared off against the wandering teachers known as Sophists in a similar contest of world views. "Man is the measure of all things: of the things that are, that they are," proclaimed Protagoras, the first and greatest Sophist. Every question has two sides. There is no truth. Appearance is reality. Whatever a person thinks is good, is good as long as he thinks it. Manipulate the world to your own advantage, they preached. Everything is relative, subjective, arbitrary.

Moral Differences Among Killings Require Different Responses

Socrates and his disciple, Plato, relentlessly battled the Sophists, insisting on absolute values, permanent and unvarying truths, difficult to discern, but ultimately real and knowable. Good and evil—justice and equality exist apart from the human mind. Today's death penalty supporters share a conviction that real moral differences exist among killings. The modern consensus that a planned torture murder is worse than an accidental killing feels like it must have been true forever. To the orator Demosthenes 2,500 years ago, it felt that way, too. Why should we punish deliberate crime but not accidents? "Not only will this be found in the (positive) laws, but nature herself has decreed it in the unwritten laws and in the hearts of men." Human beings probably always knew intuitively that some killings were worse than others. Recognizing that accidents do happen brings a feeling of restraint, nearly as primal as the urge for retaliation. These objectively different types of killings deserve different responses not because society says so. Rather society says so because the types really are different.

Pursuing moral refinements while they administer the ultimate punishment in a deeply flawed system, today's death penalty Platonists embrace Socrates' amalgam of humility about substance and also his confidence in the method. Like Socrates, we first collect instances that almost all would agree are the worst of the worst. Next, we examine these cases to find common qualities, or the essential characteristics they share. . . .

Today's Sophists—who for centuries have been calling themselves utilitarians—attack retribution as irrational. The rational person—the rational policymaker—looks only to the future, comparing costs and benefits. Punishment rehabilitates if possible, incapacitates when necessary but, in any case, primarily deters. Utilitarians today continue to make capital punishment a question of cost and benefit. They consult public opinion exclusively for what is just. Does the majority support the death penalty? If so, let's have it—if not, let's not. Man is the measure.

Morals Matter

Rejecting deterrence and public opinion polls as ultimately beside the point, many abolitionists and nearly all retributive advocates insist that there is a moral fact of the matter—

transcendent, real, and divorced from present practice. Most abolitionists know—not merely believe, but feel certain—that the death penalty is undeserved and inhumane even if 90% of the people support it. Most proponents also feel certain—independently of public opinion—that capital punishment is necessary and just. Ironically, then, retributive advocates and abolitionists ultimately never can reconcile precisely because they share this anti-Sophistic commitment to real, transcendent moral facts.

Today, almost everybody on all sides of the debate embraces another Sophistic article of faith—progress. Mores may differ in different societies, and people may be persuaded to change their views arbitrarily but, in the long run, human history progressed.

Protagoras' paradoxical faith in real progress, while denying objective values, commands the allegiance of our Supreme Court. "Time works changes," a majority declared in *Weems v. U.S.* (1910). "Cruel and unusual" was "progressive, and is not fastened to the obsolete, but may acquire meaning as public opinion becomes enlightened by a humane justice." The Eighth Amendment "must draw its meaning from the evolving standards of decency that mark the progress of a maturing society," Chief Justice Earl Warren famously declared in *Trop v. Dulles* (1958). For the past half-century, the Court unanimously has agreed that the Eighth Amendment must cause and reflect this progress.

Differences and Equal Protection Under the Law

Abolitionists anticipate the progressive limitation and eventual elimination of the death penalty. Retributivist advocates also believe in progress. Certain truths may be transcendent and timeless, but society's understanding of these moral facts and practices that reflect this awareness do evolve and improve. Platonists, motivated by a belief in the possibility of progress and an obligation to achieve it, thus continue to search for moral categories that more nearly result in homicides being classified correctly and killers more nearly getting what they deserve.

In his famous funeral oration, the great statesman Pericles declared that, in Athens, "Everybody is equal before the law." Equal treatment—*isonomia*, the watchword of the ancient Athenians—is an ideal at the very core of Western humanism. The United States long has embraced the ideal of equal protection under the law. Legislatures, the people's representatives, purportedly enact neutral death penalty statutes, to be applied by prosecutors and judges, equally to all. Any class-based death penalty, any racially discriminatory death penalty, as defined or administered, violates our commitment to equality before the law.

Yet, robbery felony-murder—the aggravator that has put more people on death row than any other—has a definite race/class effect, regardless of the legislatures' intent. If the killer's "pecuniary motive" correctly (as it commonly does) aggravates a murder, how are we to justify the tolerance and respect shown to ranking corporate executives who consciously maintain deadly workplaces, or manufacture unnecessarily lethal products from the best of motives—profit? These "red collar killers" are morally indistinguishable from other mass murderers who, with a depraved indifference, kill unsuspecting innocents. Yet, these pillars of the community rarely are indicted, almost never imprisoned and, of course, not executed for their uncaring mass murder. Unless we respond to hired killers as hired killers of whatever social class—if we fail to reflect this essential egalitarianism in the definition, detection, prosecution, and punishment of murder—we will have confirmed the Sophist Thrasymachus' definition of justice as nothing more than "the interest of the stronger." . . .

Retribution and Revenge

Seeking to impose limits, to moderate unlimited anger at each particular murder and measure it instead against the worst possible, retributivist death penalty advocates resist the "kill-them-all" set, so bent on revenge they would indulge in limitless rage. At the same time, they also resist the abolitionists for whom death always is disproportionate, no matter how heinous the murderer. When it comes to homicide, restraints must be imposed on unlimited rage to ensure limited and proportional righteous indignation. Is this possible?

Most of us painfully remember from high school geometry how Pythagoras proved the diagonal of a square was "incommensurable" with its sides. He discovered that pi and the square root of two were real, but not rational, thus destroying his whole rationalist philosophy. Those who celebrate only reason and ratio today disparage nonrational factors, not amenable to precise measurement. How much should we count "the voice of your brother's blood," or the intensity of the victim's suffering, or the killer's cruelty when it is so much easier, and more "objective" to count the number of bodies or a defendant's prior convictions? Retributivists know intuitively, however, that, although these emotive gradations are real, they are neither strictly rational nor discretely measurable.

Rationality and the Calculus of Justice

Thus, retributive death penalty advocates reject as incomplete utilitarian rationality with its future-oriented calculus of costs and benefits. No strictly rational death penalty law can be constructed and applied exhaustively to achieve justice. We need a richer language that includes nonrational, informed emotion. Moral desert never can be reduced strictly to reason, nor measured adequately by rational criteria. Forgiveness, love, anger, and resentment are part of justice. The past counts. Not rationally, but really. . . .

In *Furman v. Georgia* (1972), a majority [of the Supreme Court] ushered in the modern era of capital punishment by striking down as haphazardly administered and therefore "cruel and unusual" all the death penalties across the U.S. Absolute discretion apparently produced arbitrariness resulting in the execution of a "capriciously selected random handful." Scrambling to meet the constitutional objection of *Furman*, many states put forth detailed, death penalty codes that guided the jury and limited capriciousness. Some states fully embraced the mathematical ideal of Thales and Pythagoras enacting mandatory death penalty statutes which specified in writing all the factors—and only those factors—which, once found, automatically resulted in punishment by death. . . .

"Simultaneous Pursuit of Contradictory Objectives"

Two streams of cases have flowed from *Furman*. One requires consistency, based on aggravators clearly defined by the legislature and regularly applied in practice. The other requires that each offender be considered individually, as a concrete, but complex, unique human being. Together, these doctrines simultaneously seem to prohibit, yet require, a jury's absolute discretion. The entire modern capital jurisprudence rests on illogic—a "simultaneous pursuit of contradictory objectives," [Supreme Court] Justice Antonin Scalia complains. Heraclitus would have delighted in this contradiction and simultaneous truth of opposites, but Heraclitean "logic" was to Aristotle what the Supreme Court's jurisprudence is to Scalia and likeminded critics—simply "absurd."

In a world where logic strictly is limited to nonemotional rationality, the attack seems persuasive. Choosing between life and death, after all, involves a single decision. If examined through this strictly rational lens, death penalty jurisprudence—demanding fairness and consistency—does appear internally incoherent.

Retributivist supporters of the death penalty need to show how both core values can be respected simultaneously—how we can generally treat like cases alike and, at the same time, respect the uniqueness of each particular defendant. Heraclitus, Pythagoras, Plato, and Aristotle show us the way. Pythagoras' proof of incommensurability had demonstrated that rationality, discreteness, and propotionality were too limited for a moral universe. As the real numbers are incommensurably richer than mere rationales, so, too, capital justice, requiring nonrational emotion cannot be exhausted by written rules of law.

In capital trials, first the guilt phase narrows the class of death-eligible offenders rationally and factually, according to general criteria. The sentencing phase which immediately follows, however, assesses more than guilt. More than conduct, it measures character. Because the debate during the modern era of the death penalty has taken place almost exclusively on a rational plane, it has failed to use real but nonrational language of moral intuition to explain the particular justice of desert.

The Need for a Transcendent Concept of Justice

It may sound mystical and new age to insist that reason does not—and cannot—exhaust the inquiry. Yet, the need for a transcendent concept of justice that reconciles general consistency with the defendant's particular humanity was neither new age nor mystical to Aristotle, the rationalist, nor to Plato, his teacher. . . .

The Death Sentence as a "Reasoned Moral Response" to the Evidence

The [Supreme] Court, by and large, has united to imprison itself on a rational plane. Fearing that hatred cannot be bridled and once admitted inevitably must burst into uncontrollable rage, the Court has sought to suppress emotion. The dead victim's relatives are allowed their grief and public soundbites of fury. A grim detached rationality is expected of the rest of us, including the jury that decides the killer's fate.

Thus, in *California v. Brown* (1987), the Supreme Court held that, when deciding life or death, a jury strictly may be prohibited from being "swayed by mere sentiment . . . sympathy, or passion." Attempting to resolve the conflict between fairness and consistency, Justice Sandra O'Connor issued the Court's new watchword: The death sentence must be "a reasoned moral response" to the evidence. Sentencing was "a moral inquiry into the culpability of the defendant, and not an emotional response to the mitigating evidence" she maintained, as if it ever could be moral if it were not also partly emotional.

The Law Has Its Limits

Can we conceive, much less put into practice, a death penalty regime that provides "fairness and consistency"? Plato and Aristotle, who revered the law as rational—"the intellect without the passions"—felt forced to concede the limits to rules and rationality. Thus, in *Ethics*, Aristotle gave the West "equity, not just in the legal sense of 'just' but as a corrective of what is legally just. Not all things are determined by law. . . . For where a thing is indefinite, the rule by which it is measured is also indefinite and shifts with the contour." It is, in short, "adapted to a given situation." As Aristotle emphasized repeatedly, we cannot discover, nor should we demand, the same precision in ethics as in science. "It is not easy to determine what is the right way to be angry, and with whom, and on what grounds, and for how long."

Should society be angry at rapists who murder and mutilate children? How angry? For how long? Most important, as Aristotle asked, "What is the right way to be angry?" Straggling to deny emotion, in the end, Aristotle found nowhere else to turn but to the jury—passionate and unregulated—for that necessary supplement to "reasonable consistency" which makes true moral justice possible. In deciding between life and death, we need an incommensurably richer language to express, and a particular nonrational human faculty to assess character and desert.

Moral Intuitions Must Involve Emotions

Abolitionists and advocates during our modern era who have fought valiantly to maintain consistency and fairness must understand—must feel—that in that final stage where the jury goes with its gut, moral intuition must and should be partly emotional. Increasingly, in our own times, moral philosophers both for and against the death penalty realize this. We should acknowledge the inevitable, and declare legitimate the inescapable role of emotion. Fairness and consistency, mercy and justice require it.

Aristotle was right. We cannot expect the same degree of accuracy in moral as in scientific questions. The categories can and should be narrowed, and the jury can be made to feel its responsibility to separate the legal question (Is this murder death-eligible?) from the moral question (Does this murderer deserve to die?). Once law and equity are brought together, once we explicitly allow informed emotion—moral intuition, that innately human sense—our jurisprudence on which that condemnation rests becomes explicable and coherent.

Legal justice—rule-bound consistency—is what we demand of the jury at the guilt phase of a capital trial. Legal discretion must be limited and guided at this stage by well-defined homicide distinctions, defenses, affirmative defenses, and other factors that can be applied rationally and consistently. When it comes to the penalty phase, however, where character and not conduct is the issue, each defendant's unique personality and background assume center stage. Them, the ancient Greeks teach us, we seek fairness. "Equity"—the moral truth, based in the jury's intuition—is that mysterious rich mix of reason and emotion that combines to determine whether a person really, not merely rationally, deserves to die.

Use of the Death Penalty Cannot Be Civilized

Christopher Brauchli

Christopher Brauchli is a Boulder, Colorado, lawyer and a political columnist. In the following article, he argues that there are clear differences between the administration of the death penalty in different countries—he uses the examples of stoning in Nigeria versus the use of lethal injection in the United States—but says that in the end, "dead is dead." Brauchli also maintains that while that lethal injection seems like a "humane" method of execution, and has served in the United States to make the death penalty more palatable to society, it in fact causes the victim excruciating pain.

"Hanging was the worst use a man could be put to."

Sir Henry Wotton,
The Disparity Between Buckingham and Essex

The death penalty has once again made news. October 10 [2003] the European Union marked the first World Day Against the Death Penalty by calling for the worldwide abolition of the death penalty. The United States is in the company of, among others, Iran and Nigeria in using the death penalty to modify people's behavior. It is, of course, more civilized in its use than Nigeria so some may dislike lumping the two together. On the other hand, dead is dead.

Stoning in Nigeria

The difference between the two countries was highlighted by Nigeria's Amina Lawal, a single mother sentenced to death for having had a baby out of wedlock. She was to be executed in

Christopher Brauchli, "Dead Is Dead: There Is No Civilizing the Death Penalty," *Counterpunch*, October 22, 2003. Reproduced by permission.

a far less humane method than that employed in places such as Tennessee. She was to be buried up to her neck in sand and pelted with stones until dead. (Nigeria's highest court overturned her sentence not because it was inhumane but because she had not been observed when conceiving the child and was not given adequate time to understand the charges against her.)

Lethal Injection in the United States

Although stoning is not favored in the United States, a report in the *New York Times* on October 1 [2003] discloses that contrary to popular belief, people who are executed by lethal injection are not as happy as the drugs they are given cause them to appear.

Lethal injection was introduced because death by gassing was considered unpleasant and resulted in occasional misbehavior by those being executed. The most notable case occurred in Arizona when the recipient of the gas made obscene gestures at the onlookers while dying, thus spoiling the event for the onlookers. Shortly thereafter Arizona switched to lethal injection. What we learned on October 7 [2003] is that lethal injection is not as pleasant as all but those having first hand acquaintance with it, thought.

People who have watched someone being killed by lethal injection have observed that those being sent on their way appear as tranquil as those in a hospital room whose lives are being preserved by the most modern techniques known to civilized people. That is in part because one part of the cocktail that is administered to the soon to be departed is the chemical, pancuronium bromide, known by the trade name, Pavulon.

The Way Lethal Injection Works

Pavulon paralyzes the skeletal muscles but not the brain or nerves. Thus, people receiving it cannot move or speak nor can they let onlookers know that contrary to appearances, what is happening is no fun at all. A Tennessee judge, Ellen Hobbs Lyle, commenting on the use of the drug in an appeal brought by someone on death row in that state, said Pavulon has no "legitimate purposes." Writing about the drug's use she said: "The subject gives all the appearances of a serene expiration when actually the subject is feeling and perceiving the excruciatingly painful ordeal of death by lethal injection. The Pavulon gives a false impression of serenity to viewers, making punishment by death more palatable and acceptable to society."

Sherwin B. Nuland, a professor in the Yale medical school when told of use of the drug expressed surprise. He said: "It strikes me that it makes no sense to use a muscle relaxant in executing people. Complete muscle paralysis does not mean loss of pain sensation." He said, in effect, that there were other ways of humanely killing people. I'm sure he's right, but there are 28 states that use the same cocktail in the execution chamber as Tennessee. The first drug administered is sodium thiopental, used to induce anesthesia for a short period. It is followed by pancuronium bromide which paralyzes the patient and finally potassium chloride which stops the heart and is said to cause excruciating pain if the victim is conscious.

The Same Drug Outlawed for Use on Animals

It would be easy to simply condemn Tennessee for being a state that lacks respect for human life. That would be a mistake. Tennessee has a law that is known as the "Nonlivestock Animal Humane Death Act." Nonlivestock is defined to include pets, captured wildlife, exotic and domesticated animals, rabbits, chicks, ducks and potbellied pigs. Tennessee law says: "A nonlivestock animal may be tranquilized with an approved and humane substance before euthanasia is performed." The law then provides that "any substance which acts as a neuromuscular blocking agent, or any chamber which causes a change in body oxygen may not be used on any nonlivestock animal for the purpose of euthanasia."

The unfortunate thing, as far as those facing the executioner's needle in Tennessee is concerned, is that humans are excluded from the definition of "nonlivestock animals." Thus, the requirement for a humane execution that is imposed on those killing animals is not imposed on those killing humans. Tennessee is not alone in being more concerned about kind executions of nonlivestock animals than humans.

The American Veterinary Medical Association has come out against using the product when euthanizing animals when it is used alone or in combination with sodium pentobarbital. According to a 2000 report from the Association, "the animal may perceive pain and distress after it is immobilized." That might almost be enough to convince some people that what's good for the potbellied pig should be good for a human. On the other hand the potbellied pig is killed for what it is rather than what it did. That probably explains the more humane treatment.

Support for the Death Penalty Is Declining

Tony Mauro

Tony Mauro is Supreme Court correspondent for Legal Times, *American Lawyer Media, and law.com. In the following article he shows how the current climate in the United States regarding the death penalty is much as it was in 1972, when the Supreme Court ruled that capital punishment was unconstitutional. (That ruling was overturned four years later.) Today, Mauro says, abolitionists hope that the momentum is on their side, as the justices' concerns about the fair administration of the death penalty deepen. However, he does not see any indication of a clear majority on the Court to overturn the 1976 ruling. But he does believe that the challenges to the constitutionality of the lethal injection method will do much to temporarily halt executions, giving the justices further pause and softening existing support for the death penalty.*

Criticism of capital punishment is mounting. States are executing fewer death row inmates. Two new Republican appointees have joined the Supreme Court. But other justices are palpably uncomfortable with the death penalty.

The year was 1972.

It was the year when the Court suddenly declared the death penalty unconstitutional in *Furman v. Georgia*—a "constitutional earthquake," one commentator said at the time.

Today, in the wake of a batch of conflicting Supreme Court decisions on the death penalty this past term, abolitionists are beginning to draw parallels with that period more than a

Tony Mauro, "Death Penalty Disquiet Echoes Earlier Time," *Legal Times*, www.law .com, July 12, 2006. Reproduced by permission.

third of a century ago, when the Court's long-standing sup-
port for capital punishment dissolved, at least for a while.
(The Court allowed states to resume executions in *Gregg v.
Georgia* in 1976.)

Justices' Concerns Over the Death Penalty Are Deepening

"The Court is increasingly concerned about error in capital
cases—error that raises fundamental concerns about reliability," says Bryan Stevenson, executive director of the Equal Justice Initiative, who has been representing Alabama death row
inmates on appeal for nearly 20 years. "The doubts and criti-
cisms are beginning to echo the concerns of *Furman*."

The parallel with 1972 may reflect a good dose of wishful
thinking; some of the decisions of this past term supported
states seeking to limit inmate appeals, and executions have
certainly gone forward. In *Furman*, five justices viewed capital
punishment as unconstitutional, creating a slim but bankable
majority. On the current Court, by contrast, the number of
justices expressing serious doubts may have maxed out at
four—especially since Samuel Alito Jr. replaced Sandra Day
O'Connor in January.

In several votes on capital cases, says Kent Scheidegger of
the Criminal Justice Legal Foundation, "Alito seems to be less
inclined than O'Connor to fine-tune state procedures." Scheidegger, a capital punishment supporter, adds that he is "not
concerned" by the qualms of a minority of justices.

But this term those four justices—John Paul Stevens, David
Souter, Ruth Bader Ginsburg and Stephen Breyer—made it
clear that their concerns, especially about the possible execution of the innocent, are deepening. Their mood guarantees
turmoil ahead on the issue, with Justice Anthony Kennedy in
his characteristic role as swing vote.

On June 26 [2006] the four joined in a strongly worded
dissent in *Kansas v. Marsh*, expressing moral disapproval of a

state law that imposes a death sentence even when mitigating and aggravating circumstances are equal.

Such a scheme does not reserve the death penalty for the "worst of the worst," Souter wrote in the dissent, which quoted *Furman*. Beyond that, he said the Kansas law does not take into account the "new body of fact"—namely, the increase in the number of exonerations of death row inmates.

"In the face of evidence of the hazards of capital prosecution, maintaining a sentencing system mandating death when the sentencer finds the evidence pro and con to be in equipoise [counterbalance] is obtuse by any moral or social measure," Souter wrote.

Veteran Supreme Court advocate Donald Verrilli of [national law firm] Jenner & Block says "that level of disquiet is very significant. It's as close as they have come to saying the whole enterprise is too fraught with the risk of error."

The dissent in *Marsh* puts those four justices "very close to where Justice Blackmun left off," adds Virginia Sloan, president of the Constitution Project, which has launched a bipartisan initiative seeking ways to fix the death penalty system. In his last year on the Court the late Justice Harry Blackmun, who had dissented in *Furman*, ended his support for capital punishment. "I feel morally and intellectually obligated simply to concede that the death penalty experiment has failed," Blackmun wrote in *Callins v. Collins* in 1994.

Washington and Lee University School of Law professor David Bruck, a longtime advocate in death row appeals, says: "There seem to be four justices who have really had it with the death penalty experiment. But that's not to say that if they had a fifth vote, they would necessarily abolish it altogether."

A Degree of Innocence

The new mood of high court doubt about the death penalty has been fueled by years of revelations about death row inmates being freed based on DNA and other evidence, says

Barry Scheck, a co-founder of the Innocence Project and a former president of the National Association of Criminal Defense Lawyers. "That is what is rocking the foundation of the system."

As evidence, Scheck points to several decisions this term—not dissents—in which the Court lent support to exoneration efforts. In *House v. Bell*, the Court said that, based on strong DNA evidence, defendant Paul House should be allowed to proceed with a federal habeas appeal even though his claim was procedurally defaulted. In *Holmes v. South Carolina*, Alito's maiden opinion, the Court struck down an evidence rule that barred introduction of proof of third-party guilt.

And yet, reflecting the Court's mixed feelings about the death penalty, Scheck saw firsthand that these seemingly helpful decisions are not going to bring a swift end to executions.

Scheck invoked both *Holmes* and *House* in an eleventh-hour appeal on behalf of Tennessee inmate Sedley Alley on June 27. Alley claimed new evidence, including DNA, would prove his innocence in a case of rape and murder in 1985. But the Court denied Alley's petition, and early on the morning of June 28 he was executed.

"I thought it was a clear case for them to take," says Scheck. "It was the bitterest disappointment I can remember."

Alley's fate is a reminder that the Court is still far from turning away from the death penalty. This term the Court also decided *Oregon v. Guzek*, upholding a state rule that limits the ability of a defendant to offer innocence evidence at sentencing. In *Brown v. Sanders*, the Court upheld a death sentence even though two of the sentencing factors weighed by the jury were declared invalid.

And then there was the majority opinion in *Kansas v. Marsh*, which gave states leeway in how aggravating and mitigating circumstances are weighed. Justice Antonin Scalia chimed in with a concurrence dismissing Souter's concerns about executing the innocent.

"It is a certainty that the opinion of a near majority of the United States Supreme Court to the effect that our system condemns many innocent defendants to death will be trumpeted abroad," Scalia wrote. "For that reason, I take the trouble to point out that the dissenting opinion has nothing substantial to support it." He proceeded with an uncharacteristic outside-the-record attack on the innocence movement. "The dissent makes much of the new-found capacity of DNA testing to establish innocence. But in every case of an executed defendant of which I am aware, that technology has confirmed guilt," Scalia wrote. "In identifying exonerees, the dissent is willing to accept anybody's say-so. It engages in no critical review, but merely parrots articles or reports that support its attack on the American criminal justice system."

Fuel for Injections

At a practical level, the death penalty decision that may halt the most executions—at least temporarily—is *Hill v. McDonough*, issued June 12, which said that challenges to the constitutionality of the lethal injection method can proceed as civil rights claims under 42 USC 1983. On July 5 the Court rejected an Arkansas request to dissolve a stay of execution for Don Davis. Awaiting execution, Davis had challenged the state's lethal injections in light of the *Hill* case. Davis never made the trip to the execution chamber. Similar challenges have halted executions in Missouri and California.

These delays may be short-lived, as states are devising new chemical formulas and procedures to make this form of execution less painful. Under the prevailing three-drug sequence now in use in executions, critics say that while a paralyzing drug may make death seem painless, it may in fact be excruciating.

But Jenner & Block's Verrilli, one of the lawyers for Florida inmate Clarence Hill, says the decision was one more sign of the unease justices—including swing vote Kennedy, who wrote the *Hill* decision—have with the death penalty. At oral argument, when there was banter about old age as an alternative method of execution, Kennedy sternly cut off the discussion: "This is a death case. It was not that amusing."

Says Verrilli: "The enormous moral gravity of the death penalty, and the risk of error, are really weighing on him."

Stevenson believes that over time, similar concerns will weigh on Alito and Chief Justice John Roberts Jr., as well. Neither has had much exposure to death penalty cases. Fewer than 20 executions have taken place in Alito's 3rd Circuit in the past 30 years. Roberts handled none on the D.C. Circuit, though as a private attorney he helped represent a Florida death row inmate pro bono.

Their support for capital punishment could soften as late-night appeals come into the high court week after week, Stevenson predicts. "It's not until you are on the Supreme Court for several years that you get a feeling for how problematic and vexing the death penalty is. After a while you get exhausted and say, 'We should be doing better.'"

The Supreme Court May Alter Its Stance on the Death Penalty

Benjamin Wittes

Benjamin Wittes is an editorial writer at the Washington Post. *In the following article, he argues that there is an attitudinal shift on the Supreme Court regarding the death penalty because of questions about its unfair administration. Although Wittes does not think it is likely that the Court will strike down capital punishment once and for all, he does foresee greater constraints on its use and thinks that individual capital cases will receive greater scrutiny.*

Is it just my imagination, or has there been a palpable change recently in the Supreme Court's approach to death-penalty cases?

The Court has without question shifted gears on capital punishment. For years the justices turned a willfully blind eye to the claims of those on death row. They created onerous procedural obstacles to federal review of state convictions. They tolerated the most grotesque incompetence by counsel in capital cases, along with alarming disparities in the way the death penalty was implemented. They allowed executions not only of the mentally retarded but of the seriously mentally ill. In short, the message from the Court to death-penalty states was simple: Godspeed.

But lately the Court has struck a very different tone; one question raised by John Roberts's nomination is whether this trend will last. In two particularly high-profile cases, one in 2002 and the other last spring [2005], it rejected the death

Benjamin Wittes, "The Executioner's Swan Song?" *The Atlantic Monthly*, October 2005, pp. 42–44. Reproduced by permission of the author.

penalty first for the mentally retarded and then for juvenile offenders: the justices had upheld it in both situations as recently as 1989. In other cases the justices have also tightened the rules concerning apparent efforts by prosecutors to strike African-Americans from capital juries. They have made clear that juries, not judges, must make death judgments. They have beaten up on Texas—the nation's unrivaled leader in death-penalty activity—for cases involving flawed jury instructions and prosecutorial misbehavior. And they have sought to rein in certain lower courts that have reviewed death cases with particular leniency. It has almost seemed to be a different Court.

Justices Kennedy and O'Connor Express Doubts

Why? It was the same group of justices until now.

In large measure the shift emanates from a change of heart in what were the Court's two swing justices: Anthony Kennedy and the [now retired] Sandra Day O'Connor. Once solidly part of the bloc that deferred to state convictions and procedures, both evidently had second thoughts. Back in 1991, for example, O'Connor wrote the Court opinion refusing to even consider the case of Roger Keith Coleman, a Virginia death-row inmate with particularly strong claims of innocence. Coleman had lost his chance to appeal when his lawyers missed a state-court filing deadline by a single day. O'Connor began the opinion. "This is a case about federalism." A decade late, however, she was singing a different tune. "Serious questions are being raised about whether the death penalty is being fairly administered in this country," she said in a 2001 speech in Minnesota. "Minnesota doesn't have it, and you must breathe a big sigh of relief every day."

Kennedy's shift has been just as dramatic. In 1989, for example, Kennedy signed Justice Atonin Scalia's opinion upholding the death penalty for people who committed their offenses as juveniles. This year he wrote the opinion striking down the juvenile death penalty, and in doing so he explicitly repudiated several of the methodological premises of the Scalia opinion he had signed.

The attitudinal shift on the part of Kennedy and O'Connor—two of the less rigidly principled justices in recent years—is hardly a surprise. As DNA exonerated growing numbers of prisoners through the 1990s, the public grew more skeptical toward capital punishment in general, realizing that even when juries are sure of a person's guilt, they are sometimes dead wrong. Although polls still show majority support for the death penalty, that support is shrinking. Juries are handing down fewer death sentences. Executions countrywide, after reaching a modern-day high of ninety-eight in 1999, declined to fifty-nine last year. Judges are not immune from the anxieties that have led to these trends. It would actually be surprising if no Supreme Court justice had rethought his or her approach in light of what we now know about capital punishment.

The Future of the Death Penalty

So is the Court getting ready to strike down the death penalty once and for all?

Almost certainly not. And for the Court's reticence on this point, foes of the death penalty (of which I am one) should, paradoxically, count themselves lucky. The justices went down the abolition road once before. In their ill-fated 1972 decision in *Furman v. Georgia*—which came down at a time when capital punishment was on the decline anyway—they effectively struck down the death-penalty statutes of every state in the country that had them. The intense public reaction against the decision provoked many states to rewrite their capital-punishment laws to comply with the Court's new standards— much as the current backlash against judicially mandated recognition for gay marriage is prompting state constitutional amendments that limit marriage to heterosexual couples. Within just a few years the Court allowed these new laws to go into effect: executions began again—and then sky rocketed, from one in 1977 to twenty-five in 1987 to seventy-four in 1997. By denying the public the option of a penalty that, although disfavored by elites, was supported—then as now—by much of the policy at large, the courts intensified public commitment to it. With capital punishment once again on the wane, justices uncomfortable with it would be deeply foolish to repeat that mistake. Even the Court's liberal flank seems to understand this.

Scrutinizing Capital Cases

So is the new judicial scrutiny in capital cases just window dressing?

Not at all. The Court's new interest in scrutinizing capital cases has the effect of reducing the death penalty's political air supply—that is, of constricting its public legitimacy. In theory this should not be the case—just as the permissive attitude the Court for many years took toward executions should not have functioned as a political enabler of them. The Court has never approved of or rejected the death penalty as a political matter. Its decisions merely outline what the ground rules of democratic government require of states that want to use it. Yet people do not read Supreme Court opinions in strictly legal terms. Every time the Court upholds a dicey state conviction, it sends a message legitimizing capital punishment. In contrast, when the Court nibbles away at the death penalty, it undermines its acceptability. It also makes capital cases ever more difficult and expensive for states to litigate thereby making capital punishment progressively less viable as a regular instrument of criminal justice.

Such moral and practical constraints may not matter in Texas, Oklahoma, and Virginia, where the death penalty is a comparatively routine feature of the criminal-justice system.

But states like these are the exception, not the rule: only five states have accounted for two thirds of all executions since 1976. In most places where the death penalty is legal it is quite marginal, and judicial tolerance can matter a lot to its vitality. Recently, for example, courts in New York effectively invalidated that state's death-penalty statute, which had been passed only in 1995 and had never led to an execution. The state legislature decided not to pass another.

Fair Representation and Change of Personnel

What are the big issues to come?

The most important is quality of counsel, about which the blitheness of the Court's jurisprudence has bordered on the obscene. The Fifth Circuit Court of Appeals recently had to debate, for example, whether under the Supreme Court's precedents a death-row inmate whose lawyer had slept through considerable portions of his capital trial was presumptively entitled to a new trial. The Court has issued a few opinions recently—including a potentially significant one last term—emphasizing the importance of effective counsel. But it has only begun to tinker with its prior approach here, and it's far from clear that the justices intend a real revision. Even in the midst of their newfound concern about capital cases, for example, they let a Virginia man be executed despite the fact that, unbeknownst to him, his lawyer at trial had previously represented the person he was accused of killing. No state behavior in capital cases as consistently undermines fair-trial rights as the appointment of ill-prepared, overworked, or just plain lousy lawyers to represent people whose lives are on the line. How seriously the justices take on this question will tell a lot about how committed they are to a new approach.

How much will the change of personnel affect the Court's direction here?

71

Perhaps a lot. If Roberts proves hard-line. O'Connor's resignation could shift doctrine back toward permissiveness very quickly. On the other hand, a Bush appointee to replace Chief Justice William Rehnquist—a solid part of the Court's conservative flank on these questions—wouldn't have to be very moderate to fortify the current trend considerably.

New Constraints on the Death Penalty

So what's your instinct about where all this is headed?

Despite O'Connor's retirement, the Court's new approach seems likely to impose significant constraints on capital punishment, but ones that will be largely invisible to the public. The Court will probably not be striking down many laws, but the justices will tighten the screws by scrutinizing individual cases enough to further isolate the death penalty regionally and to raise its political and financial costs. This is a matter less of politics than of simple human nature. The Court speaks in the language of principle, but only a few of the justices are so committed to the principle of deference to state-court judgments that they would feel comfortable over time seeing their names on opinions upholding manifest injustices. Since Roger Keith Coleman's execution, in 1992, Virginia law-enforcement authorities have successfully resisted calls for posthumous DNA testing that could resolve his claims of innocence. Coleman may or may not have been innocent but someday we're going to learn for sure that someone put to death in this country was in fact not guilty. And it's a fair bet that no one would want her obituary to say she called the debate over that execution "a case about federalism."

CHAPTER 2

The Death Penalty
as a Crime Deterrent

Statistical Evidence Shows That the Death Penalty Is a Deterrent

Paul H. Rubin

Paul H. Rubin is professor of economics and law in the Department of Economics at Emory University. In the following article, he presents his findings from studying the empirical data regarding the deterrent effect of capital punishment. He says that previous studies comparing murder rates in states with and without the death penalty were problematic, and that a more appropriate approach is to look at statistical evidence. He and his colleagues analyzed the murder rates during the years the death penalty has been legal and compared them to the rates during the four-year moratorium on capital punishment, from 1972 to 1976. He maintains that the evidence points to executions having a clear deterrent effect on homicides, saying that each execution led to between eight and twenty-eight fewer murders.

Many arguments can be made for or against the death penalty. Many of them focus on aspects of morality: Is it just for the state to kill someone? Should a murderer suffer a punishment similar to the loss of his victims? Is "an eye for an eye" still appropriate, or is it barbaric?

I will not consider any of these arguments. I will not even argue a position with respect to the death penalty, or capital punishment. Rather, I will analyze the issue as an economist and ask the following questions: What are the consequences of an execution? Will an execution have the effect of deterring other potential murders, or will it merely satisfy some desire for vengeance? That is, I will examine the best evidence available on the question of deterrence. When I have discussed this evidence, readers will be in a position to make their own decisions as to the merits of capital punishment. One cannot make an informed decision without knowing the consequences.

History of Deterrence Research

The question of deterrence has long been at the forefront of the debate on capital punishment. Theoretical arguments exist on both sides. Those arguing against deterrence claim that murders are not sufficiently rational to calculate probabilities or respond to incentives, or that murders are committed in the heat of passion and murderers do not consider the consequences. Those making the opposite argument claim that humans are generally rational and respond to incentives, and that criminals are not fundamentally different from others in such qualities. Among the major proponents of the latter view is [economist] Gary Becker, the Nobel Laureate in economics who, in a famous article published in 1968, argued that criminals respond to changes in conditions in about the same way as everyone else.

Because theory cannot definitively answer the question of the existence of deterrence, analysts have turned to empirical or statistical methods. Among the first to use such analysis on the question of the deterrent effect of capital punishment was [sociologist] Thorsten Sellin. In a 1959 book, Sellin compared states with and without capital punishment and found no significant difference in homicide rates. His methodology is improper, as I show below, but it is still used by some analysts: the *New York Times*, in an article published on September 22, 2000, used exactly this methodology.

Cross-state comparisons present two problems. First, they do not hold enough factors constant in a statistical sense. That is, even states that appear "similar" can differ in many ways that are relevant for determining the homicide rate, and a gross comparison of murder levels by state cannot adjust for these differences. For example, murder rates have been shown to respond to differences in incomes, racial composition, age of the population, and urbanization and population density. The probability of arrest is also a significant factor, and can also vary across states. A simple state-by-state comparison cannot capture these many differences. The only way to adjust for these multiple factors is to use a multivariate statistical tool such as some variant of multiple-regression analysis; simple two-by-two comparisons such as those used by Sellin and the *New York Times* are inadequate. (Sellin was writing before the statistical and computational tools were available to perform the sort of analysis required; the *New York Times* has no such excuse.)

The second reason for the inappropriateness of state-by-state comparisons is that causality can go either way. That is, a state may have capital punishment precisely because it has a higher murder rate and is trying to control this evil. In such a case, observing capital punishment and a high murder rate says nothing about causality, and the deterrence argument is that rates would be even higher if there were no capital punishment.

The first serious attempts to examine these influences in a modern statistically valid model were made by Isaac Ehrlich, a student of Gary Becker. In two papers published in the 1970s, Ehrlich examined the effect of executions on homicides, one at a national level and one at the level of states. In both he found a statistically significant deterrent effect. However, others have reanalyzed his data extensively and have found no such effects. Statisticians and econometricians have had a very active debate over this issue, using Ehrlich's data.

In 1972 the U.S. Supreme Court imposed a moratorium on executions, which was lifted in 1976. From the perspective of this article, the effect of the moratorium was that for four years no data was available to extend the data used by Ehrlich.

Moreover, even when the moratorium was lifted, relatively few executions took place because states had to pass new statutes and determine whether these were acceptable to the Court. It was not until 1984 that more than five executions occurred in any given year in the entire United States. To date, no published study has used this data to analyze the question of deterrence.

Our Research

Along with two colleagues at Emory University (Hashem Dezhbakhsh and Joanna Mehlhop Shepherd), I have performed a statistical analysis of this data. Our analysis has several advantages over previous analyses. First, we have used county-level data, rather than national or state data. The advantage of county-level data is that populations are more homogeneous within counties, so statistically the results are more accurate. Moreover, there are more than 3,000 counties in the United States, so there is a large amount of data. This large amount facilitates statistical analysis. Second, we use techniques (called "panel data") that were not available when Ehrlich did his research. Moreover, these techniques require large amounts of data, which again are available for the county-level analysis. Thus, we are able to advance the argument significantly because we have more and better data and better statistical techniques than were available to others.

A multiple-regression analysis such as that which we perform essentially estimates homicide rates as a function of demographic and other characteristics of the jurisdiction (here, the county). The analysis then can implicitly calculate the effect of each execution on the number of homicides that would otherwise have occurred.

In performing this analysis, we had to solve an important problem. We are interested in the effect of an increase in the probability of an execution on homicides. But a probability must be calculated with a denominator. The probability of an

77

execution is the number of executions divided by the number of homicides. But it is necessary to determine the appropriate year for the number of homicides to put in the denominator. It appears that there is now an average lag of six years between commission of a murder and execution. That is, if an execution occurs in 2001, but the crime was committed in 1995, how do we measure the probability? Does the execution in 2001 deter murders in 1995, or in 2007, or for some year in between? To account for this difficulty, we used three measures of the lag structure. We also used two methods of adjusting for missing data. Thus, we ended with six equations measuring the deterrent effect of executions.

In all six cases, we found that each execution led to a significant reduction in the number of homicides. The most conservative estimate (that is, the one with the smallest effect) was that each execution led to an average of eighteen fewer murders. The "95 percent confidence interval" estimate for this value was between eight and twenty-eight fewer homicides. In other words, we can be 95 percent sure that each execution resulted in at least eight fewer homicides, and it is likely that each execution actually deterred more than eight homicides. All other estimates were even larger than this.

Implications

As I mentioned above, the existence of a significant deterrent effect does not prove that capital punishment is good or socially desirable. But it does indicate that if we decide not to execute murderers, then we are making a decision that will lead to many additional murders in society.

Critics of capital punishment raise numerous issues. I will consider one such issue here: the issue of race. Critics claim that African Americans are more likely to be executed than are whites. This may be true. But there are two relevant factors. First, U.S. Department of Justice figures show that African Americans are much more likely to commit homicide than are others. Secondly, and more importantly, African Americans are also more likely to be victims of homicides. For 1999, for example, homicide victimization rates per 100,000 persons were 3.5 for whites and 20.6 for blacks. For that year, there were 7,757 white and 7,134 black homicide victims. Thus, when an execution deters murders, many of these deterred murders would have been of African Americans.

The Death Penalty Does Not Deter Crime

Ted Goertzel

Ted Goertzel is a professor of sociology at Rutgers University. In the following article, Goertzel discusses the question of whether executing people lowers the homicide rate or not. He says that social scientists have arrived at varying conclusions on this question because each of them uses different research methods. Comparative studies show there is no deterrent effect of capital punishment, while econometric models show a mixture of results. Goertzel discusses several studies on capital punishment using comparative studies and econometric models. He says economists who advocate studies based on statistics make the mistake of thinking that messy social realities can be turned into tidy mathematical proofs. His view is that research methods with good qualitative data and little statistical manipulation show that the death penalty is not a deterrent against murder.

> I have inquired for most of my adult life about studies that might show that the death penalty is a deterrent, and I have not seen any research that would substantiate that point.
>
> *Attorney General Janet Reno, January 20, 2000*

> All of the scientifically valid statistical studies—those that examine a period of years, and control for national trends—consistently show that capital punishment is a substantial deterrent.
>
> *Senator Orrin Hatch, October 16, 2002*

It happens all too often. Each side in a policy debate quotes studies that support its point of view and denigrates those from the other side. The result is often that research evidence

Ted Goertzel, "Capital Punishment and Homicide: Sociological Realities and Econometric Illusions," *Skeptical Enquirer*, vol. 28, July–August 2004, pp. 23–27. Copyright 2004 Committee for the Scientific Investigation of Claims of the Paranormal. Reproduced by permission.

is not taken seriously by either side. This has led some researchers, especially in the social sciences, to throw up their hands in dismay and give up studying controversial topics. But why bother doing social science research at all if it is impossible to obtain accurate and trustworthy information about issues that matter to people?

There are some questions that social scientists should be able to answer. Either executing people cuts the homicide rate or it does not. Or perhaps it does under certain conditions and not others. In any case, the data are readily available and researchers should be able to answer the question. Of course, this would not resolve the ethical issues surrounding the question, but that is another matter.

So who is right, Janet Reno or Orrin Hatch? And why can they not at least agree on what the data show? The problem is that each of them refers to bodies of research using different research methods. Janet Reno's statement correctly describes the results of studies that compare homicide trends in states and countries that practice capital punishment with those that do not. These studies consistently show that capital punishment has no effect on homicide rates. Orrin Hatch refers to studies that use econometric modeling. He is wrong, however, in stating that these studies *all* find that capital punishment deters homicide. In fact, some of them find a deterrent effect and some do not.

But this is not a matter of taste. It cannot be that capital punishment deters homicide for comparative researchers but not for econometricians. In fact, the comparative method has produced valid, useful, and consistent findings, while econometrics has failed in this and every similar area of research.

The first of the comparative studies of capital punishment was done by Thorsten Sellin in 1959. Sellin was a sociologist at the University of Pennsylvania and one of the pioneers of scientific criminology. He was a prime mover in setting up the government agencies that collect statistics on crime. His method involved two steps: First, a comprehensive view of the subject which incorporated historical, sociological, psychological, and legal factors into the analysis in addition to the development of analytical models; and second, the establishment and utilization of statistics in the evaluation of crime.

Sellin applied his combination of qualitative and quantitative methods in an exhaustive study of capital punishment in American states. He used every scrap of data that was available, together with his knowledge of the history, economy, and social structure of each state. He compared states to other states and examined changes in states over time. Every comparison he made led him to the "inevitable conclusion . . . that executions have no discernable effect on homicide rates."

Sellin's work has been replicated time and time again, as new data have become available, and all of the replications have confirmed his finding that capital punishment does not deter homicide. These studies are an outstanding example of what statistician David Freedman calls "shoe leather" social research. The hard work is collecting the best available data, both quantitative and qualitative. Once the statistical data are collected, the analysis consists largely in displaying them in tables, graphs, and charts which are then interpreted in light of qualitative knowledge of the states in question. This research can be understood by people with only modest statistical background. This allows consumers of the research to make their own interpretations, drawing on their qualitative knowledge of the states in question. . . .

In a comparison of homicide rates per 100,000 population in Texas, New York, and California, from 1982 to 2002, Texas executed 239 prisoners, California ten, and New York none. The trends in homicide statistics are very similar in all three states, all of which follow national trends. These states were chosen arbitrarily, but data for other states are readily available. If you prefer to compare Texas to Oklahoma, Arkansas, or New Mexico, the data are readily available in back issues of the *Statistical Abstract of the United States* and *Uniform Crime Reports*. The results will be much the same.

Hundreds of comparisons of this sort have been made, and they consistently show that the death penalty has no effect. There have also been international comparative studies. [Sociologists Dane] Archer and [Rosemary] Gartner (1984) examined fourteen countries that abolished the death penalty and found that abolition did not cause an increase in homicide rates. This research has been convincing to most criminologists, which is why Janet Reno was told that there was no valid research linking capital punishment to homicide rates.

The studies that Orrin Hatch referred to use a very different methodology: econometrics, also known as multiple regression modeling, structural equation modeling, or path analysis. This involves constructing complex mathematical models on the assumption that the models mirror what happens in the real world. As I argued in a 2002 *Skeptical Inquirer* article, this method has consistently failed to offer reliable and valid results in studies of social problems where the data are very limited. Its most successful use is in making predictions in areas where there is a large flow of data for testing. The econometric literature on capital punishment has been carefully reviewed by several prominent economists and found wanting. There is simply too little data and too many ways to manipulate it. In one careful review, [economist Walter] McManus found that: "there is much uncertainty as to the 'correct' empirical model that should be used to draw inferences, and each researcher typically tries dozens, perhaps hundreds, of specifications before selecting one or a few to report. Usually, and understandably, the ones selected for publication are those that make the strongest case for the researcher's prior hypothesis."

Models that find deterrence effects of capital punishment often rely on rather bizarre specifications. In a rigorous and comprehensive review [economist Samuel] Cameron observed that, "What emerges most strongly from this review is that obtaining a significant deterrent effect of executions seems to depend on adding a set of data with no executions to the time series and including an executing/non-executing dummy in the cross-section analysis ... there is no clear justification for the latter practice."

In less technical language, the researchers included a set of years when there were no executions, then introduced a control variable to eliminate the nonexistent variance. The other day upon the stair, they saw some variance that wasn't there. It wasn't there again today, thank goodness their model scared it away. Not all the studies rely on this particular maneuver, but they all depend on techniques that demand too much from the available data.

Since there are so many ways to model inadequate data, McManus was able to show that researchers whose prior beliefs led them to structure their models in different ways would obtain predictable conclusions: "The data analyzed are not sufficiently strong to lead researchers with different prior beliefs to reach a consensus regarding the deterrent effects of capital punishment. Right-winger, rational-maximizer, and eye-for-an-eye researchers will infer that punishment deters would-be murderers, but bleeding-heart and crime-of-passion researchers will infer that there is no significant deterrent effect."

The Death Penalty Will Not Deter Terrorism

Thomas McDonnell

Thomas McDonnell is a professor at Pace University School of Law in White Plains, New York. In the following article he asks whether the United States should impose capital punishment on those involved in acts of terrorism against its institutions and its people. He says that if anyone deserves the death penalty, such mass murderers do. However, the threat of the death penalty is not likely to deter similar actors in the future, and in fact the death penalty might actually encourage such actors because, if caught, they can still be martyrs after being executed by the U.S. government.

A federal jury from the conservative Eastern District of Virginia has denied Zacarias Moussaoui his apparent wish—to become a martyr at the hands of the United States. The only person convicted in the United States of Sept. 11, 2001–related crimes and sometimes called the Barney Fife of al Qaeda, Moussaoui seems to have done all he could have in the sentencing trial to guarantee a trip to the death chamber.

Contradicting his previous accounts, Moussaoui testified in the first part of the trial against the advice of his lawyers, claiming for the first time that he and failed shoe bomber Richard Reid were to fly a plane into the White House on 9/11 and that he lied to FBI agents upon his arrest, precisely what the government had been arguing to justify a death sentence. (Moussaoui, himself, had been in jail for 26 days on 9/11.) During the second part of the trial, Moussaoui openly and repeatedly mocked the families of the 9/11 victims, saying he regretted that more Americans had not been killed.

Thomas McDonnell, "Death Penalty Won't Deter Terrorism," *New Jersey Law Journal*, June 5, 2006. Copyright 2006 American Lawyer Media L.P. © 2006 ALM Properties, Inc. This article is reprinted with permission from New Jersey Law Journal.

Four days after Moussaoui was sentenced to life without possibility of parole, after the jury could not unanimously agree on a death sentence, he moved to withdraw his guilty plea. He [claimed] that he lied at trial about his involvement in 9/11. U.S. District Court Judge Leonie Brinkema summarily denied his motion.

Moussaoui's strange case invites an examination of whether we should Impose capital punishment on those involved in acts of terrorism against the United States, its institutions and its people. If anyone deserves the death penalty, those who planned and actively participated in the 9/11 conspiracy do. The United States will almost certainly execute such participants, including Mohammed Shaikh Khalid, Ramzi bin al-Shibh and Abu Zubaydah, assuming that it chooses to try them and they are found responsible, as expected, for the 9/11 attacks.

Yet after more than four years in the "war on terrorism" have passed, a grudging recognition is beginning to arise that we need the United Nations, the help of our allies and respect for the rule of law. Similarly, the natural demand for retribution after a terrorist organization has committed mass murder and other heinous crimes needs to be tempered by the fact that carrying out the death penalty may strengthen the terrorists.

Because 19 hijackers were willing to kill themselves to carry out the 9/11 crimes and because al Qaeda and its related organizations continue to use suicide bombers, the threat of the death penalty is not likely to deter similar actors in the future. In fact, in a perverse way, the death penalty might actually encourage such actors. If caught, they can still be martyrs after being executed by the U.S. government.

Given the perceived and actual grievances that the Arab and Islamic worlds have toward the West in general and the United States in particular, carrying out such executions may tend to inflame the Arab and Islamic worlds, increase their support of terrorist movements and thwart cooperation with our allies, almost all of whom have abolished the death penalty. U.S. attorneys can argue, however, that even if suicide bombers may not be generally deterred, and even if executing terrorists causes some repercussions, those with any responsibility for the 9/11 attacks, the worst crimes ever committed on American soil, warrant the death penalty.

As Lord Justice Denning stated, "The truth is that some crimes are so outrageous that society insists on adequate punishment, because the wrong-doer deserves it, irrespective of whether it is a deterrent or not."

Yale Law Professor Charles Black observed, however, that the death penalty is an evil, because, among other things, "it extinguishes, after untellable suffering, the most mysterious and wonderful thing we know, human life; this reason has many harmonics." Such harmonics may include strengthening support in the Arab and Muslim world for al Qaeda and its related groups and disciples. So instead of clinging to capital punishment, we will probably do better by turning off the klieg lights [bright spotlights] of the death penalty theater.

Despite the jury's conclusion in its somewhat contradictory special verdict that the defense had failed to establish Moussaoui's potential martydom as a mitigating factor [Judge] Brinkema, in sentencing him, told Moussaoui what rejecting the death penalty signified: "You came here to be a martyr and to die in a big bang of glory, but, to paraphrase the poet T.S. Eliot, you will die with a whimper."

CHAPTER 3

Is the Death Penalty Fair?

The Unfair Administration of the Death Penalty

Dave Lindorff

Dave Lindorff is an award-winning investigative reporter and a regular columnist for CounterPunch. *In the following article, Lindorff shows that sentencing errors, usually the result of incompetent or inadequate defense attorneys, often wrongly send inmates to their death, even after the mistakes are discovered and ruled unconstitutional. While the death penalty is supposed to be applied to the worst of the worst offenders, he says, often this is not the case. And a capital-sentencing error, like murder itself, casts a wide net of suffering, impacting the family of the accused and offering little closure to the victims' families, who sometimes wait decades for the executions to take place.*

May 6, 2005. Dobie Gillis Williams was picked up in a police roundup after a woman was stabbed to death in her bathroom in rural Louisiana in 1987. With an IQ of 65, and a lawyer who was subsequently disbarred for incompetence, Williams was tried for murder, convicted and sentenced to death. He twice came within hours of execution, only to have the process stayed, first by the U.S. Supreme Court and a second time by the governor.

A federal judge finally overturned Williams' sentence, citing two errors: Williams had confessed only after a police officer promised Williams he wouldn't get the death penalty, and his attorney never offered any evidence of mitigating circumstances during the sentencing phase of his trial—evidence that should have included Williams' mental deficit and a childhood of abuse and neglect.

Dave Lindorff, "Unjust Executions," Salon.com, May 6, 2003. This article first appeared in Salon.com, at http://www.Salon.com. An online version remains in the Salon archives. Reprinted with permission.

But Williams was executed anyway in 1999, when the notoriously pro-death-penalty 5th Circuit Court of Appeals (which serves Louisiana, Mississippi and Texas) overturned the district court judge's decision, ruling that the revelation of errors came too late under the 1996 Effective Death Penalty Act (EDPA). Williams' appellate attorney, Nick Trentacosta of the Louisiana Center for Equal Justice, maintains that his client's execution was in error. The fact that mitigating evidence hadn't been presented to the jury wasn't in dispute—just the timing of when that issue had first been raised on appeal.

Williams, whose case might seem unique in its disastrous outcome, was hardly unusual. Nobody has yet come up with an irrefutable example of an innocent person having been executed since states began reinstating the death penalty in 1976, but even death penalty advocates concede that sentencing errors in death penalty cases have led to the execution of many criminals who, by law, should not have received the ultimate sanction.

"There are definitely plenty of sentencing errors, where those who die haven't deserved to die," says Robert Blecker, a self-described "staunch advocate" of the death penalty who teaches criminal law at New York Law School. Blecker, who believes that errors work both ways—with people who should, in his view, be executed getting off—adds that the main cause of wrongful executions is inadequate counsel and the failure to present mitigating evidence to the jury.

And, he says, such sentencing errors "tend to happen most often in cases where those who die don't really deserve to die." In the most heinous murders, he claims, sentencing errors are rare. Appellate courts have found sentencing errors in more than 40 percent of all capital cases since 1973—when the Supreme Court ruled the existing death penalty statutes unconstitutional—but there are no figures to indicate how many inmates were executed or remain on death row due to sentencing errors. Steven Hawkins, a staff attorney with the National Coalition to Abolish the Death Penalty, estimates that "at least 40 to 80" of the 800 people executed since 1977 "were probably victims of obvious error, such as failure to have mitigating circumstances raised at trial." An equal number, he adds, were "simply victims of the U.S. Supreme Court's failure to make various death penalty rulings retroactive" for all condemned inmates.

That last condition—essentially, the stubborn upholding of fatal errors by the courts—is remarkable, given the stakes. The decision to apply rulings exclusively to future cases, largely to avoid disrupting legal precedents, is typical of the U.S. Supreme Court. Most often, it is barely noted. But in death penalty cases the procedure has enormous impact. When a sentencing error has been exposed, often as an unconstitutional element of existing law, but not applied retroactively, it means that those on death row as a result of the same unconstitutional law will not be spared—unless their case was specifically part of the appeal that brought the ruling.

Just last year, for instance, the Supreme Court ruled it was unconstitutional for death penalties to be determined by trial judges. Rather, the court held, that decision belongs to juries alone. Yet a number of condemned men—in states such as Alabama, Arizona, Colorado, Delaware, Florida, Idaho, Indiana, Montana and Nebraska—have subsequently been executed after being sentenced to death by judges—sometimes, as in the case of Alabama, Delaware, Florida and Indiana, by judges who actually overruled juries that had recommended a lesser sentence. More prisoners, with older cases, are still being sent to their unconstitutional death. In fact, this is true for many, if not most, of the Supreme Court's more far-reaching death penalty decisions.

The same holds for lower court decisions. In December 2001, a federal District Court in Pennsylvania overturned the death sentence of death-row prisoner Mumia Abu-Jamal, on the grounds that his jury in 1982 had been provided with a sentencing form so confusing that it appeared to require all 12 jurors to agree to a mitigating circumstance before any one of them could consider it in deciding whether Abu-Jamal deserved the death penalty or life without parole.

Abu-Jamal, a journalist and former Black Panther convicted of killing a white policeman, came within days of being executed back in 1995 because of this error, but he was spared when his appeal hearing ran past the execution date, voiding it. In fact, Pennsylvania, like most other states with death penalty statutes, says that if any juror finds a mitigating circumstance, that juror may consider that factor in deciding between life or death. (Since a death sentence must be decided unanimously by a jury, just one juror voting against death results in a life sentence instead of execution.) Yet despite the reality that many of the 244 other people on Pennsylvania's death row were sentenced by juries using the same confusing form, no blanket order revoking those sentences was issued following the ruling in Abu-Jamal's case.

Jim Liebman, a professor of law at Columbia University, is the lead author of two recent studies of death penalty errors, which surveyed virtually all the death penalty cases in the country since the Supreme Court reinstated capital punishment in the mid-1970s. He points out that the highest rates of sentencing error are consistently found in states such as Arizona, Nevada or Pennsylvania, all of which have very "broad" death penalty statutes—that is, statutes that allow for capital punishment for a wide variety of crimes—while a state like Colorado, which has a very narrowly applied death penalty, has far fewer errors.

In reviewing all 5,760 death sentences issued between 1973 and 1995, Liebman says he found that 41 percent—about 2,360 cases—had been tossed out on appeal because of "sentencing errors." Among those, more than 300 were overturned on initial appeal by a state court on the grounds that the so-called aggravating circumstance (a finding required for imposition of the death penalty) in fact did not exist. A third were overturned at the post-conviction phase or by a habeas appeal on grounds of "ineffective counsel" (most often for failure to introduce mitigating evidence at a sentencing hearing). Another 19 percent were overturned because of the suppression of exculpatory evidence by prosecutors.

Subsequent to their sentences or convictions being overturned, 82 percent of capital defendants have received lesser sentences—a figure that leads Liebman to conclude that "they were oversentenced in the first place."

Liebman notes that sentencing errors are also likely to be common among the 59 percent of capital cases in which the convictions were not reversed on appeal.

While public debate and media attention about the death penalty have focused on wrongful convictions, "sentencing errors go to the heart of the problem with the death penalty," Liebman argues. "The idea of the death penalty is that it is supposed to be applied to the worst of the worst offenders, but this is not what is happening." He adds that "hundreds of cases of sentencing error" have gone uncorrected, including many that have already led to executions. Agreeing with Blecker, he adds, "The marginal cases are where most of the errors turn up."

Advocates of capital punishment, for the most part, express little concern about sentencing errors. "Just about anyone would agree that the execution, or for that matter just the incarceration of an innocent person, is of far greater concern than the execution of a person who is actually guilty, of premeditated murder," says Kent Scheiddegger, of the Criminal Justice Legal Foundation, a pro-capital-punishment organization based in California. "I don't think that the execution of a person who has committed premeditated murder is an injustice. The worst it can be is an uneven dispension of mercy."

Others see the matter differently. "Even if it is someone who is a killer, we're still talking life and death," Liebman says. "I don't think we can be so callous as to say, 'They're killers, so who cares if they live or die'—especially since you see people with resources getting their sentences overturned and others without resources going on to execution."

Besides, not everyone sent to death row is guilty of premeditated murder. Take Phillip Tompkins, a borderline mentally retarded black man convicted of killing a woman in Texas after deliberately colliding with her car and then taking her to a secluded spot to rob her. According to prosecutors, Tompkins tied the woman, Mary Berry, to a tree, stuffed part of a bedsheet in her mouth, and then left to use her ATM card and steal $1,000. An all-white jury found that Tompkins had murdered her, but it was never clear whether he had intended to do so, particularly given his low IQ.

Manny Babbitt suffered the same fate. A decorated Vietnam War veteran (he was awarded his Purple Heart on San Quentin's death row only weeks before his death), Babbitt was executed in May 1999 for the death of Leah Schendel, a 78-year-old woman who died of a heart attack in 1980 during Babbitt's attempt to burglarize her home. No claim of premeditated murder was made by the state. Rather, it became a death penalty case because of a California law making death caused in the process of a burglary a capital offense.

Babbitt's state-appointed trial attorney—who was later disbarred for financial improprieties—failed to introduce mitigating evidence of his client's prior confinement in a mental hospital, or of his obvious symptoms of post-traumatic stress disorder from his Vietnam experience—Babbitt had been observed reenacting battle scenes as a homeless person in Providence, R.I., prior to the burglary.

Two jurors in the Babbitt case subsequently testified that had they known of his wartime experiences and mental history, they would not have voted for death. His subsequent execution, which followed a rejection by Gov. Gray Davis of his clemency appeal (which had been endorsed by hundreds of Vietnam vets), also illustrates how capital-sentencing error, like murder itself, casts a wide net of suffering.

"When my Manny was sentenced to death, at first I thought of killing myself," recalls his older brother Bill, 60, who personally turned in his brother after word of Schendel's death, on a promise by the police that his brother would not receive a death sentence. "I turned Manny in because I felt sympathy for that family, and I felt very guilty about it when they went ahead and sought the death penalty."

Bill Babbitt, now active with the group Murder Family Victims for Reconciliation, says that his brother's 17 years on death row, and his ultimate execution, were "devastating" to his family, which included himself, a mother, two children and several grandchildren. While saying he feels great sympathy for the victim's family, he ask, "What kind of closure did they have? They could have had closure in 1982 if Manny had been sentenced to life in prison. The prosecutors told them that when Manny was dead, they'd feel better. Instead, the state kept that wound open almost 20 years. That's closure?"

Bill Babbitt watched, along with several of Schendel's relatives, as his brother was killed by injection. "Her granddaughter couldn't watch," he recalls. "She looked at the floor. So did the prosecutor. But I watched the whole thing. My brother had told us he was not afraid to die, and that we should not show any malice toward the victim's family. He said he would keep his eyes closed and meditate on God and Jesus, but that he wanted a smiling face watching him. So I told him I'd be there."

Liebman says that since sentencing errors are so often the result of incompetent or inadequate defense attorneys, they are often red flags for probable errors in the guilt phase of the trial—suggesting that some of those with sentencing errors may well have been wrongfully convicted too. "It's just that sentencing errors are much easier to prove," he explains.

That is because while guilt must be proven "beyond a reasonable doubt," the standards for justifying the death penalty are much lower. "In the conviction phase of a capital trial, the whole burden of proving guilt is on the prosecution, so you pretty much have to prove the errors occurred there, which is harder to do," says Liebman. "In the sentencing phase, part of the burden is on the defense—to bring in mitigating evidence to convince a jury that death is not appropriate. If an attorney doesn't do that, it's easy to point it out on appeal."

That doesn't mean an appeals court will go along with a claim of ineffective counsel, however. Even in cases where defense attorneys slept through trials or attended while stone drunk, higher courts have upheld the subsequent convictions and death sentences of their hapless clients. But at least it is relatively easier to present evidence that no mitigating evidence was submitted than to prove that a conviction was incorrect.

Liebman adds it is also politically easier for judges in capital cases to overturn a sentence that leaves a convict behind bars for life than to overturn a conviction, which raises the possibility that the individual might end up back on the street. At the same time, he says it is clear that, since the reinstatement of the death penalty in the United States nearly three decades ago, hundreds of capital prisoners have already been executed whose sentences were in error.

That certainly was the case with Robert Coe, the only prisoner to be executed in Tennessee since the reinstatement of the death penalty in that state. Coe, executed in 2000, was a severely mentally ill individual with a grotesque history of abuse as a child—his father raped his sister in front of him and had punished him for a childhood transgression by deliberately shooting him in the leg.

While there were serious questions about whether Coe was even guilty of raping and killing a young girl—the police found bloody sheets in the room of a prosecution witness whom the defense argued might have been the real killer, but they "lost" the evidence before testing the blood—what is beyond debate is that Coe's public defender, like Dobie Gillis Williams' attorney, never introduced any mitigating evidence during his sentencing hearing. The jury never heard that he had been institutionalized in Florida for severe schizophrenia, nor did jurors hear anything about Coe's history of child abuse at the hands of his father—evidence that ought to have mitigated against a death sentence.

Attorneys brought into the case late in Coe's appeal to the federal courts tried to introduce the mitigating evidence, but the federal courts, bound by the strictures of the Effective Death Penalty Act of 1996, held that it was "too late" for such evidence to be considered. They ruled that Coe's original trial attorney and his first appellate attorneys had erred in not introducing that evidence at the state court level, and that it was thus "procedurally barred." (In an all too common Catch-22, the court also held that the seemingly outrageous error of not introducing readily available mitigating evidence was not sufficient evidence of ineffective counsel.)

As in Williams' case, a federal district judge did temporarily lift Coe's death sentence on the grounds of an erroneous jury instruction, but a three-judge panel of judges in the 6th Circuit Court of Appeals overturned that ruling on a 2-1 vote, and Coe was executed.

"The state of Tennessee decided to execute a mentally ill person. They knew he was mentally ill and that he had been an abused child, but they decided to go forward with Tennessee's first execution in 40 years," says the Rev. Joe Ingall, who came to know Coe during his years of incarceration on death row. "This case was all about the politics of death, not about justice. They needed to kill somebody, so they killed Robert."

After years of clamping down on death row inmates' right of appeal, the Supreme Court seems to have lightened up in recent months, making capital-punishment cases a little harder to win and a little easier to challenge. Besides its ruling that juries alone can vote for a death sentence, the court more recently lowered the standard of proof for death row inmates seeking to claim that their jury panels were unconstitutionally purged of minority jurors. The court also criticized the 5th Circuit Court of Appeals and lower federal courts in the district for accepting without question the rulings and procedures of state courts in death penalty cases, suggesting that "technicalities," which can be life-or-death matters in capital cases such as Coe's and Williams', while an important aspect of American jurisprudence, are not clear-cut matters of fact.

Finally, the court ruled that retarded people should not be executed, though it left unresolved how lower courts should determine what constitutes retardation.

But capital-punishment critics like Liebman, and even death penalty advocates like Blecker, argue that the problem of errors, in both the guilt and sentencing phases of capital cases, will continue to plague the system, at huge cost—both psychological and financial—to society and to inmates, and to the families of victims and inmates.

"Everybody loses," says David Elliott, a spokesman for the National Coalition to Abolish the Death Penalty. "Remember that people on death row have relatives, and those relatives are losing a loved one. And the victim's relatives have to live through years of trials and hearings. And then there's the prisoner," he adds. "If he's executed because of a sentencing error, that's terrible, but even if the error is eventually corrected, he has lived under the threat of death for years. We have seen these people, and afterwards many of them have something resembling post-traumatic stress disorder. They can't adjust to the reality that they aren't going to die."

Both Liebman and Blecker suggest that the quickest way to reduce these errors would be to ensure that all capital murder defendants are provided the resources to put on an adequate defense, and for legislatures and prosecutors to narrow the range of crimes that allow for a death penalty.

But mandating adequate defense counsel in capital cases is costly, and in most states, the burden of financing first-class defense counsel and appellate counsel for capital cases would fall on already strapped local governments. Raising taxes is always a hard sell. Raising them in order to help capital defendants beat the rap, or to help convicted killers contest their convictions or their sentences is an even harder sell. Yet critics of the system say something has to be done.

"When you have a death penalty system, and you start diluting it by executing people who don't deserve to die while not executing others who do, it means the system is breaking down," says Liebman. "What's needed is more honesty about what's happening. We have to have a commitment to get rid of all the error."

Juvenile Offenders Should Be Eligible for the Death Penalty

Thomas R. Eddlem

Thomas R. Eddlem is a conservative commentator and radio talk show host in Southeastern Massachusetts and a frequent contributor to The New American *magazine. In the following article, he discusses the Supreme Court decision in March 2005 that declared it unconstitutional to impose capital punishment for crimes committed while under the age of eighteen. Eddlem says the Court in fact had a duty to uphold the death penalty for juvenile offenders, and in overturning it did not stay true to the U.S. Constitution. In the article Eddlem also describes Justice Antonin Scalia's outrage in his dissenting opinion on the case, expresses his disapproval at the court's citing of foreign sources on the main text of its decision, and criticizes what he sees as the Court's arrogance in stepping beyond its legal bounds.*

Supreme Court Associate Justice Antonin Scalia is known for using some acerbic terms in his opinions, but his dissent in the 5-4 decision *Roper v. Simmons*, which purported to declare that the death penalty for anyone under 18 years of age is "unconstitutional," took the cake. In the course of saying that the majority opinion had "no foundation in law or reason." Scalia used the terms such as "mockery," "usurpation," "diktat," and "sophistry." For usually reserved language in court decisions, this was the Supreme Court equivalent of Scalia throwing his chair at the other justices.

What caused such a furor? At the bottom of the majority decision in *Roper v. Simmons* was the claim that the execution of anyone who had not reached his 18th birthday constituted "cruel and unusual punishment" under the Eighth Amendment to the U.S. Constitution (as "incorporated" on the states by the 14th Amendment.) Christopher Simmons, the Simmons in *Roper v. Simmons*, was seven months short of age 18 when he committed his heinous crime. He broke into his neighbor's house, kidnapped the elderly woman, hog-tied her with duct tape and electrical wire, then threw her off a bridge while she was still alive and conscious. He boasted beforehand that he would be able to get away with his crime because he was a minor. Though the court had explicitly ruled in the 1989 case *Stanford v. Kentucky* that the execution of the 16- and 17-year-olds was not "cruel and unusual punishment," the five majority justices arrived at the opposite conclusion on the basis of examining social data from across the United States and throughout the world and supposedly finding a "consensus" of opinion in what they called "evolving standards of decency that mark the progress of a maturity society." "This data gives us essential instruction," the majority opinion claimed. "We then must determine, in the exercise of our own independent judgment, whether the death penalty is a disproportionate penalty for juveniles."

In opposition, Scalia noted that the traditional view of the Anglo-American common law system was that "the concept of 'law' ordinarily signifies that particular words have a fixed meaning. Such law does not change...." The majority's reliance on dubious opinion surveys—in contravention of the clear language of the Eighth Amendment and laws enacted by popularly elected state legislature—means that the words in the Eighth Amendment no longer have any meaning beyond the backdrop of a contrived "consensus" asserted by a majority of justices. "Since [the majority of the Supreme Court justices] are not looking at the same text, but a different scene," Scalia explained, "why should our earlier decision control their judgment?"

International "Confirmation"

Of particular concern to constitutionalists is the majority's increasing reliance on international opinion for its own deci-

sions. "Our determination that the death penalty is disproportionate punishment for offenders under 18 finds confirmation
in the stark reality that the United States is the only country
in the world that continues to give official sanction to the juvenile death penalty," the majority found calling "the laws of
other countries and . . . international authorities . . . instruc-
tive for its interpretation of the Eight Amendment's prohibition of 'cruel and unusual punishment.'" Though the court
referenced international opinion and international treaties as
authorities in footnotes of past decisions (such as the 1998
Thompson v. Oklahoma and the 2002 *Atkins v. Virginia*), *Simmons* is the first case where the Supreme Court explicitly cited
international agreements in the main text of the decision itself.

The court noted that "Article 37 of the United Nations
Convention on the Rights of the Child, which every country
in the world has ratified save for the United States and Soma-
lia, contains an express prohibition on capital punishment for
crimes committed by juveniles under 18."

Even some liberals are aghast at the court's ruling. *Boston
Globe* columnist Thomas Oliphant, an opponent of the death
penalty, wrote on March 3 that the "implication, however, is
troubling—that basic principles in our law are affected by recent decisions in Congo, China, Nigeria, Yemen, Saudi Arabia,
Pakistan and Iran." As Oliphant says: "[The] new standard is
that the state can kill you for something you did after your
18th birthday, but you live if you committed a heinous murder at 17 years, 11 months, 29 days I'm just one person but I
don't recall that much changing in that interval."

Personal Views, Not
Constitutional Interpretation

Scalia denounced the court's internationalist perspective:
"[T]he basic premise of the Court's argument—that American
law should conform to the laws of the rest of the world—

ought to be rejected out of hand." He stressed in his dissent the court's hypocrisy in its reliance on foreign sources for its decision. "In fact the court itself does not believe it," Scalia charged pointing out that the court insists upon a much more strict "separation of church and state" (a phrase not found in the Constitution) than the rest of the world. He also cited "the Court's abortion jurisprudence, which makes us one of only six countries that allow abortion on demand until the point of viability." And he noted that if the court wants to get in line with an international "consensus" on cruel and unusual punishment, then the court didn't go far enough: "[I]n addition to barring the execution of under 18 offenders, the United Nations Convention on the Rights of the Child prohibits punishing them with life in prison without the possibility of release. If we are truly going to get in line with the international community, the Court's reassurance that the death penalty is not really needed . . . gives little comfort."

Scalia noted that the *Roper v. Simmons* decision is evidence that the court rules on the basis of nothing more than "a show of hands on the justices' current personal views." But the court does not want to advertise this power grab, and so it finds what it can—including foreign laws—to support its decisions. "To invoke alien law when it agrees with one's own thinking, and ignore it otherwise." Scalia concludes, "is not reasoned decisionmaking but sophistry."

Federal Judicial Activism

Another important constitutional principle, overlooked even by "conservative" justices such as Scalia, is that the 14th Amendment does not empower the Supreme Court to decide if *state* capital punishment laws are in conformity with the Eighth Amendment. The 14th Amendment states in part: "No State shall . . . deprive any person of life, liberty, or property, without due process of law; nor deny to any person within its jurisdiction the equal protection of the laws." The Supreme

Court has found in this wording an "incorporation doctrine," incorporating into the 14th Amendment restrictions on *state* actions, the Eighth Amendment as well as other parts of the Bill of Rights. On this basis, the Supreme Court claims that it can rule on state laws that properly should not be decided on the federal level, including in *Roper v. Simmons*, state capital punishment laws.

Of course, the intent of the post-Civil War 14th Amendment was to ensure that the states would not be able to punish anyone without a trial and that everyone, including the former slaves would enjoy "the equal protection of the laws." Moreover Congress, not the Supreme Court, was empowered to enforce the 14th Amendment. As the amendment states: "The Congress shall have power to enforce, by appropriate legislation, the provisions of this article."

Fortunately, Congress still possesses the means to halt federal judicial activism. Congress can limit the appellate jurisdiction of the Supreme Court to hear certain kinds of cases, such as capital punishment cases. Congress can also limit the jurisdictions of and even abolish if it chooses, all lower federal courts. Finally, Congress can impeach rogue justices who routinely ignore constitutional restraints. Congress desperately needs to give serious consideration to a combination of these remedies for judicial activism.

Executing the Powerless

Michael A. Wolff

Michael A. Wolff is chief justice of the Missouri Supreme Court. In the following article, he points out that in appellate courts, where court decisions are reviewed and appeals heard, jurors play an essential role in capital cases. Jurors must not be unwilling to consider the death penalty, and they decide what factors—such as mental illness and lack of mental capacity—make an offender eligible for execution. Unlike legal professionals who consider more analytical questions about the categories of people eligible for the death penalty, says Wolff, jurors face the more difficult task of deciding whether a particular individual should die.

Justice Blackmun, in the last death penalty case of his career, proclaimed that he would no longer "tinker with the machinery of death." To those of us who still tinker with the machinery of death, questions of mental capacity, culpability, and the character of the offender weigh heavily. As an appellate judge, tinkering means applying legal principles, not dealing with ultimate questions of morality, justice, and personal responsibility.

For most of the countries of the world, and a dozen states of our own country, the tinkering is an abstraction, for their laws do not include consideration of the death penalty. For the rest of us, the application of legal principles may be intellectually challenging. At the appellate level—nearly always one level removed from the question of whether an offender "should" be executed—the role seems rather dispassionate when compared with the role of prosecutors and jurors, who play an essential role in virtually every capital case.

Michael A. Wolff, "Tinkering with the Machinery of Death–Mental Capacity, Ability, and Eligibility for the Death Penalty," *Saint Louis University Public Law Review*, vol. 25, Winter 2006, pp. 279–81. Reprinted with permission of the Saint Louis University, Public Law Review © 2006 Saint Louis University School of Law, St. Louis, Missouri.

The trial courts, and in particular the citizens called to serve as jurors, are the crucial point in the process. Jurors do not write opinions; they rarely speak publicly. They are considered seriously, most often, by those who study how they may be manipulated in individual cases. Jurors are first selected only if their personal views do not preclude consideration of the death penalty. They are "death-qualified" jurors, and they are chosen to the exclusion of the substantial minority of citizens who could not in any circumstances consider capital punishment.

Upon a finding of guilt in a capital murder case, these death-qualified jurors then must weigh the aggravating and mitigating factors of the crime, and the characteristics of the offender, to determine whether there are aggravating factors that make the offender eligible for the death penalty. Even if there are aggravating factors justifying the death penalty, the jury can still say "no." This is the point in the process where moral values and personal ethics become central. Jurors consider these matters quite seriously. One could spend an entire career looking for death penalty jurors who have treated this duty cavalierly and you would probably find only a very few. Few if any jurors, I would venture to say, would describe their deliberations as "tinkering." Only a career of judging could bring forth the word tinkering; jurors would probably more likely use a more substantial word like "weighing."

My focus on the role of jurors, . . . is intended to set the stage and provide the backdrop for . . . legal and analytical questions. . . . Most deal with exclusion of categories of persons eligible for the death penalty. Why do we not execute the mentally ill, the retarded, the youthful offender? These cases carry a common notion that such offenders are not sufficiently culpable for law to authorize execution.

But why is that? Consider youthful age. In *Roper v. Simmons*, the prosecutor used offender Simmons' youthful age to argue that it was an aggravating factor, not a mitigating factor.

In effect, the prosecutor successfully argued to the jury that if Simmons was this violent and scary as a seventeen-year-old, consider what he would be like later in life. By the same principle, one could ask why we would exclude mentally ill persons. Some of them are genuinely scary and dangerous, and even the best of chemicals and consistency of treatment may not make them less so. And if I carry this argument one step further to the mentally retarded, in contemporary society I would run the risk of alienating most readers because, as the Supreme Court concluded in *Atkins v. Virginia*, there is a societal consensus that execution of the retarded is cruel and unusual.

So I return to a more interesting point, from an analytical perspective, that is, how do we determine as a legal matter whether somebody is eligible for the death penalty or whether the person is ineligible because of certain characteristics of his psyche, mental capacity, or youth?

With mental illness and lack of mental capacity, the questions involve defining the characteristics, and more importantly, determining in which cases they apply. When the law excludes execution of the mentally retarded, for instance, the more difficult question becomes whether a particular offender is mentally retarded so that he is ineligible for the death penalty.

These questions of fact, more challenging than the issues of law involved, are left to juries. Actually these questions are addressed in the first instance by prosecutors who must decide whether or not to seek the death penalty. These prosecutorial decisions are influenced, in turn, by what prosecutors think that juries will do in individual cases. What are prosecutors and juries doing? Missouri statistics tell an interesting story. The number of death sentences has dropped in the past five years. In fiscal year 2001 through 2003, there were two per year, and none in the first half of fiscal year 2004. From fiscal years 1993 through 2005, 10.9 percent of first-degree murder convictions resulted in death sentences. From 2001 through 2004, however, the percentage was about half of that average. This drop started before the U.S. Supreme Court decisions in *Ring, Atkins*, and *Simmons*. The significant effect may have come from the widespread publicity about wrongful convictions.

The consideration of the principles [focusing] on the analytical concepts . . . involves a close examination of legal principles, and the application of these legal principles to particular offenders. But it is important to consider, as we study these principles and their application, not just to consider the question: Who is he? But rather, who are we?

The Mentally Ill Should Not Be Subject to the Death Penalty

Sally Satel

Sally Satel is a psychiatrist who studies domestic drug policy, mental health policy, and political trends in medicine. In the following article, she discusses the case of Andrea Yates, who drowned all five of her children in the bathtub of her Houston home in June 2001. The prosecution insisted Yates deserved the death penalty because she was culpable for her actions, saying she made many choices in her planning of the killings and thus could not have been insane. But Satel insists that this applies a mistaken conceptual framework to the mindset of a psychotic, and that a seriously mentally ill offender should not be subject to the death penalty.

It took a little under four hours for a Texas jury in March 2002 to find Andrea Yates guilty of capital murder in the drowning deaths of three of her children. Today the jury will decide whether she gets the death penalty.

The facts of her case have been headline news since June 2001, when Yates drowned all five of her children in the bathtub of their Houston home. Within an hour after placing the lifeless bodies on her bed, Yates called the police. In the years leading up to the drownings, Yates attempted suicide twice, suffered dark depressions after her children's births, was hospitalized and treated with the anti-psychotic medication Haldol. These and other details strongly suggest that her behavior was the product of delusion—of postpartum psychosis, to be more precise.

Sally Satel, "It's Crazy to Execute the Insane," *The Wall Street Journal Western Edition*, March 14, 2002, p. A18. Copyright © 2002 Dow Jones & Company, Inc. All rights reserved. Reprinted with permission of The Wall Street Journal and the author.

Insane, Evil, or Mentally Ill?

Immediately after the killings, debate swirled around whether Yates was insane, evil or an everymother pushed to the brink by the combined demands of domesticity and child rearing. Over time, a consensus formed that she was mentally ill. Even most of those who want to see Yates on death row admit that she was profoundly sick when she killed.

Being psychotic at the time of her crime was not enough, however, for Yates to be found not guilty by reason of insanity. In Texas such a determination turns on whether the defendant knew at the time of the offense that her actions were wrong.

The prosecution argued that Yates was not insane because she made lots of choices. "She made the choice to fill the tub," prosecutor Kaylynn Williford told the jury. Her calling the police was evidence of her awareness of wrongdoing. Yates was described as "rational" when the police came to her house the day of the crime; she told them where the keys to the backdoor could be found and directed them to clean glasses when they wanted a drink of water.

The Psychology of Culpability

It is no surprise that an insane person could do these things. Just because someone is psychotic does not necessarily prevent him from doing everyday things well. I have had many patients who were very psychotic (paranoid, hearing voices, believed they were Joan of Arc) but who could still balance checkbooks and go shopping. One was very diligent at clipping and using Kmart coupons. Someone who has a very low IQ [intelligence quotient] could probably not manage these things smoothly, and people who are demented (think of an advanced Alzheimer's patient) or delirious (someone just coming out of a seizure, or heavily inebriated) cannot manage them at all.

Had Yates been retarded, demented or delirious, then it is possible she would have not realized she was committing murder. Instead she was psychotic. In my opinion, she knew exactly what she was doing, but—and this is vital to understanding her psychology—her purposeful actions were based on a deranged premise. Did she know it was wrong in this narrow sense? I suppose so, but that narrow legal sense is clinically and morally meaningless.

As she saw it, her choice was not to kill them or let them live happy lives. It was kill them or else subject them to horrifying damnation at the hands of Satan. She saw herself as a poisonous mother—in jail she wanted to shave her head to see if the 666 sign was still branded on her scalp—from whom her children should be protected. In this calculus of kill-them-to-save-them, Yates could justify her actions.

Her case is reminiscent of Russell Weston's. Another high-profile psychotic, he burst into the U.S. Capitol building in 1998 and shot to death two guards. Weston "purposefully" traveled from Montana to Washington so he could dismantle the time-controlling satellite system housed in the Capitol and thus save the world from disaster. His actions flowed logically from his beliefs, but those beliefs were unhinged.

A Mistaken Conceptual Framework

The law is impervious to these subtleties. The jury's directive—to discern whether Yates knew that killing her children was wrong—applies a mistaken conceptual framework to the mindset of a psychotic.

For the promise of a resolution we should turn to the Supreme Court's recent debate about whether the Constitution permits the execution of the mentally retarded. Of the 38 states with the death penalty, 18 prohibit the execution of the retarded. Last year alone five state legislatures outlawed the practice, and public sentiment is clearly shifting.

Mentally retarded individuals are considered "least culpable" because they cannot foresee the consequences of their deeds. In 1989 the court decided that executing the mentally retarded did not constitute cruel and unusual punishment. At that time only two states banned capital punishment for the retarded, prompting the court to say that there was not sufficient evidence of a "national consensus" that doing so violated the country's "standard of decency."

Treatment, Not Death, for the Mentally Ill

If so, standards should shift. States should not subject to the death penalty individuals like Andrea Yates who were deeply psychotic at the time they committed their crime. This is not to say they should be sent back to their homes. Here is an intriguing proposal put forth by mental health advocate D.J. Jaffe.

Sentence seriously mentally ill offenders to psychiatric treatment for the same length of time one would sentence any other offender. Half way through their sentence—which would be served in a forensic institution—they would be eligible for intensive supervised release. The supervision would almost surely include the requirement to take psychiatric medication. This would be especially valuable for individuals who, unlike Yates, did meet the standard for not guilty by reason of insanity and went on to be released from a mental hospital after only a few years without any treatment requirement.

The Supreme Court decides what is cruel and unusual based on evolving standards of decency as understood by society at large. If the Texas jury gives Yates a death sentence tomorrow, it will be a sure sign that those standards have not yet evolved as much as they should.

Age Is Not an Excuse for a Stay of Execution

Chuck Klosterman

Chuck Klosterman, a journalist, critic, and essayist, writes a regular column for Esquire *magazine. In the following essay, Klosterman discusses the issue of whether someone is too old to be executed. He focuses on the story of Clarence Ray Allen, who was executed at age seventy-six, just months following his resuscitation by state medics after suffering a heart attack. In his fight for clemency, Allen had argued that he was too old and sick to be executed, and further that the death chamber was not wheelchair-accessible. Klosterman says he is not sure whether capital punishment is the correct social response to crimes such as Allen's, but posits that the death penalty is always hard to regulate and that it is a mistake to use an offender's good behavior, age, and circumstances after the fact as a reason for not executing him.*

I suppose I have a position on the death penalty, but just barely: I think capital punishment should probably be illegal—but if we aren't going to outlaw it, we should probably use it way more often. Statistics have consistently shown that the death penalty does not work as a deterrent for murderers, but I suspect it would serve as a major deterrent for teenage shoplifters. When I enter the Pennsylvania gubernatorial race against [former football player and sports broadcaster] Lynn Swann, this will be a key plank in my platform. Nobody will ever accuse Chuck Klosterman of being soft on (non-drug-related) crime.

Like most present-day problems, the debate over capital punishment amounts to a loose confederation of ethical quan-

Chuck Klosterman, "How Old Is Too Old to Die? A Few New Wrinkles in the Death-Penalty Debate," *Esquire*, vol. 145, April 2006, pp. 88–90. Copyright 2006 © Hearst Communications, Inc. All Rights Reserved. Reproduced by permission of the author.

daries that are well-known to any adult who's ever considered a problem more complex than how to beat the Legend of Zelda. *Should society punish people by replicating the same act as the criminal? Is it irresponsible to inflict an irreversible penalty? Is vengeance sometimes a justifiable motivation?* Et cetera. Whenever people discuss capital punishment, these are the points they argue. But I've recently been thinking about a specific facet of the larger debate. My question is this: Can someone be too old to die?

Clarence Ray Allen was executed by the state of California on January 17, minutes after his seventy-sixth birthday. His lawyers fought hard for a stay of execution, and not just because their client claimed he was innocent. (Allen was originally given a life term for killing his son's girlfriend in 1974 but was later sentenced to death for orchestrating at least three more murders from his prison cell.) Allen's paradoxical argument for clemency was that he was too old and sick to be executed. He was blind and half deaf, he suffered from diabetes and he was consigned to a wheel-chair. Part of his contention was that the California death chamber wasn't wheel-chair-accessible. In essence, Allen felt he shouldn't be killed by the state because the execution would probably kill him.

In September of 2005, Allen was resuscitated by prison medics after he suffered a heart attack. This is the most intriguing twist to the story: The state of California saved Allen's life so that it would be able to kill him later. This is like having sex with someone you despise just so you can break up with her on Valentine's Day. "The People of California' are in a morbid race with God to see who can kill Clarence Ray Allen first," wrote Michael Kroll in the January 10 issue of *New America Media*, and that's a flashy little sentence. However, I think Kroll had it backward. The People of California were in a morbid battle *against* God to keep Clarence Ray

Allen alive until they could kill him on their own terms. And I don't know if this makes the People of California merciful, wicked, or insane.

What exactly is the cutoff for this kind of conundrum? Let's pretend I am an executioner for the state of California. (Perhaps I find the work a little depressing, but the benefits are great and the hours are flexible.) I am scheduled to execute an aging serial killer at 12:01 A.M. by means of lethal injection. (This is someone who has killed eight hundred innocent people, and I have no doubt about his guilt.) The inmate is being strapped to the death table, and I am methodically preparing the sodium thiopental (this is a sedative) and the pancuronium bromide (this is the paralyzing agent) and the potassium chloride (this is the toxic agent). But at 11:50, the killer goes into cardiac arrest. What is the protocol? My gut reaction would be to work *faster*, but I'm certain killing the man early would not be an option; I'd probably lose my job, I could just wait it out and see if he's still alive at 12:01, but that seems beyond medieval; nobody wants to stand around and witness an eleven-minute seizure. What (I assume) would happen is this: The prisoner would be removed from the table, rushed into the infirmary, and saved by medical personnel. The cost of this emergency treatment would be paid by the California taxpayers the murderer didn't get around to murdering. The execution would be postponed until his heart was stronger; he would then be injected with potassium chloride, which would cause cardiac arrest and kill him.

Now, I realize this scenario is wholly hypothetical and (possibly) more interesting than plausible. But it does illustrate a core problem with capital punishment: Even when you accept its existence, it's hard to regulate. As soon as death becomes part of the equation, all the other rules change—often because they suddenly become irrelevant. For example, inmates on death row are always on suicide watch. They are not allowed to kill themselves. Why? If a jury decides that someone must die on the morning of June 1, why is he *obligated* to live until May 31? This is akin to someone getting a DUI [driving-under-the-influence citation] and having his driver's license revoked for eighteen months while also being prohibited from selling his car. "The defendant's '88 Caprice Classic must remain in his garage with a full tank of gasoline," the judge would decree. "He obviously can't drive it, because that is the penalty. But he can't just *decide* to quit driving."

I do not know if Clarence Ray Allen deserved to die for his crimes: I do know that he didn't deserve to live simply because he was old. I am also unsure whether Crips founder Stanley "Tookie" Williams deserved to be executed last December for his gang-related past, but I certainly don't think he deserved to be spared because he became a nice guy during the twenty-five years he was in prison; he was sentenced to death for killing people, not for being a jerk. These situations seem to happen a few times every year: We learn of a convicted felon who was condemned to death row many years ago. At long last, the day of reckoning approaches—but the prisoner is no longer the person we convicted. He (or she, in the case of [convicted and executed murderer] Karla Faye Tucker) is now sitting in a wheelchair or quoting the Bible or writing poetry about the duality of man, and we all get nervous. Suddenly, it feels f---ed up to kill this person. But there is the truth: It's *always* f---ed up to kill people like this, or it's *never* f---ed up to kill people like this. And if thirty-eight U.S. states are willing to align themselves with the latter notion, they need to embrace the totality of that decision, even when it makes them (and us) uncomfortable.

There is a minority of Americans who hate capital punishment, and there is a minority who love it; everyone else is somewhere in the middle. By and large, the country favors it. But I've always suspected there is an unspoken fallacy among those who mildly support the death penalty. Even though they find the idea of killing people semibarbaric, they subconsciously associate capital punishment with the vague elimination of evil (almost as if the world contained a finite amount of invisible malevolence that could be slowly drained through the destruction of especially bad people). This is why cases like Allen's drive people crazy; they see a blind, deaf man who can't walk fifteen feet, and it feels like that evil is already gone.

Which doesn't matter at all.

The death penalty is not the solution to the social problem of evil; it is the social response to a specific kind of evil behavior. And it might be the wrong response. But killing the old and pathetic doesn't make it any worse.

CHAPTER 4

Personal Perspectives on the Death Penalty

Why I Stopped Supporting the Death Penalty

David R. Dow

David R. Dow is a professor of law at the University of Houston. In the following excerpt from his book about the American death penalty, Dow explains how he changed from being a supporter of capital punishment to a lawyer defending death row inmates. He says that his personal experience has showed him that the death penalty is applied unfairly, and that too often people are on death row not because of what they have done but because their cases have been mishandled. For this reason, he says, there is no such thing as a just death penalty, and it must be abolished.

When I started representing death row inmates in 1988, I was not opposed to the death penalty. I was somewhere between agnostic and mildly in favor of capital punishment. Frankly, the death penalty was not an issue I had spent much time thinking about. The question of capital punishment was, to me, an abstraction, far away from my own life. I had known two murder victims, but I did not know any murderers. I did not know how the system works.

That is no longer true. Now I know many murderers, and most of them will be executed. They will be executed not so much for what they have done, but because their lawyers failed them or because the courts refused to get involved. They will be executed not simply because they committed murder, but for technical reasons, reasons that I thought were not supposed to matter. That is the first lesson I learned as a death penalty lawyer.

This book is not a book about *the* death penalty; it is a book about *our* death penalty. Back in the days when the death penalty was still an abstraction to me, in the days before I had to prepare my clients and their families for death, I imagined that death row was populated with characters like Charles Manson and Hannibal Lecter. But Hannibal Lecter is fictional, and Charles Manson is not on death row at all. The actual inmates on death row ordinarily do not conform to the stereotype. When I realized that, the idea for this book began to grow; it developed out of a gradual recognition that my perception of the death penalty, and my perception of death row, did not even remotely resemble the reality. After the idea took shape, there was a single moment when I decided to write it.

It happened in Livingston, Texas, on a sweltering summer day in 2002. Livingston houses the Polunsky unit of the Texas Department of Criminal Justice, otherwise known as Texas's death row. The city of Livingston is on the edge of the big thicket, in East Texas. The land is fecund, crossed with rivers and creeks, and dense with cypress and pine. To get to the prison from my office at the University of Houston, I drive about seventy-five miles to the north-northeast. I see logging trucks hauling timber and farmers selling fresh produce on the side of the road, but no liquor stores: Death row sits in a dry county.

During the nearly two hours that it takes me to drive to the prison, I rehearse the conversations I will soon be having. A death penalty lawyer is part lawyer and part therapist. Every lawyer has to advise his or her client about the likelihood of prevailing, but when a death penalty lawyer tells the client that he or she will probably lose, it means that the client will be executed. Law school does not train you to have that conversation. I tell all my clients that they will probably be executed because in all likelihood they will be. Unlike a medical patient, for whom attitude might play a role in his or her recovery, my clients' fate is not affected by their good cheer. If they remain sanguine and hopeful, I do not try to talk them out of it. But I don't encourage it either, because I don't want to lie to them.

To see my clients, I pass through four electronic gates and two chain-link fences topped with rolls of razor wire. I hear a pack of dogs yapping in their kennels; they are trained to hunt down any escaped inmate (since death row was moved to its current location, no inmates have escaped). When my clients come out to see me, they are escorted to their places by a pair of guards. Their hands are shackled behind them. They sit in a cage, behind thick bulletproof glass. The guards lock the door behind them. My clients then squat on their haunches, like catchers behind a home plate, so that the guards can reach through a slot into the cage and uncuff their hands. We converse on a phone.

Across the visiting room sit vending machines with sodas, sandwiches, chips, and candy bars. If you want to buy food for the inmate you are visiting, you put coins in the machine, and a guard then puts the food into a paper bag, which she then passes to another guard, who passes it to the inmate through the same slot that was used to unshackle him. Visitors cannot touch the food or use paper money to purchase it. Only coins are permitted. The floors have eggshell-colored linoleum. The chairs are made of folding metal. There are two bathrooms, one for women and one for men, with doors that do not lock. The area is sterile and not particularly comfortable.

During the week, visiting hours last until 5 P.M. On Saturdays, death row inmates have evening visiting hours, from 5 until 9 P.M. Fridays are busy, because families can drive to Livingston for the weekend and visit their loved ones for two consecutive days without having to miss much work. On Friday afternoons, pickup trucks with camper tops crowd the parking lot, and the motels are full. In the death row visiting area, dozens of young children run around. They are the sons and daughters, brothers and sisters, of the more than four hundred people on Texas's death row.

I decided to write this book on a Friday. I try to avoid the Polunsky unit on Fridays because I do not want to see the families. But on one particular Friday in 2002 I had to be there, and what struck me was the children. I had seen them before, of course, but never really noticed them. The toddlers were playing, as toddlers do, oblivious of what was around them. Some of the older children were crying softly. I spoke briefly to an inmate who was scheduled to be executed the following week and asked whether there was anything my office could do. He said that there was not. He was a so-called volunteer, a death row inmate who does not want any appeals filed on his behalf because he would rather be executed than spend his life in a sixty-square-foot cell. At his trial, he had been represented by a lawyer who had come to the courtroom drunk and snorted lines of cocaine in the bathroom during breaks in the testimony.

As I handed the phone to his mother, I finally apprehended the chasm between reality and my previous perceptions. This man had committed a murder, but he had been remorseful from the very moment that he had done so; and he had never been violent in prison. Undoubtedly, he had done something terrible, but he did not remotely resemble the stereotypical murderer; and he was on death row not so much because of what he had done, but because the lawyer that the state had appointed to represent him was a drunk and incompetent. I handed the phone to his mother, then I watched him say good-bye, first to her, then to his fourteen-year-old son. He could not hug them or kiss them because contact visits are not allowed on death row. That was the day I decided to write this book.

People have opinions about the "big" issue: whether capital punishment is moral or immoral, whether the state should or should not be in the business of executing its citizens. But that big issue is not really relevant, because the death penalty that people debate is not the death penalty we have. The abstract questions are too big and too disconnected from reality. In this book, I focus on something smaller. I focus on individual cases because even though the abstractions are too big, we can understand the individual cases, and once we do, we can think about what they mean.

I understand—and I appreciate—the arguments for the death penalty. As I mentioned, I used to support it myself. When I stopped supporting it, it was because I realized that the death penalty is applied unfairly. There is no room to dispute that, and I hope this book will illuminate this unfairness. Some of the people I write about have committed horrible crimes, but that is not why they were executed. They were executed because the police or prosecutors were corrupt, because their own lawyers were inept, or because the judges did not do their jobs. You might think there is such a thing as a just death penalty, and perhaps there is, but even if there is such a thing in theory, our death penalty system does not come close to fitting the bill.

The difference between who I am now and who I was when I started representing death row inmates is the difference between knowing just an inmate's name and knowing an inmate, between knowing how the system is supposed to work and how it actually works. In this book, I tell you how the system actually works. I introduce you to some of the cases—and some of the people—that have changed my views. You will learn how a death penalty agnostic became convinced that the only defensible position regarding the death penalty is to abolish it.

A Chaplain Learns to Forgive Murderers

Gary Egeberg

Gary Egeberg is a teacher, spiritual guide, and former California state prison chaplain. In the following article, he explains that his experiences during his years as a prison chaplain led him to support the death penalty when he had previously been against it. But, he says, after he left the prison system, meditation, biblical study, and an understanding of inmates' moral development led him to reverse his position once more.

When I left the Twin Cities in June 2002 to begin my service as a lay Catholic chaplain in a California maximum security prison housing 5,000 male inmates, I had no idea what to expect other than warmer weather. I certainly didn't expect to find myself changing my position on the death penalty. I didn't expect to go from being against it to being for it. To be honest, I was a little bit embarrassed to find my heart hardening and my mind closing, especially so quickly.

I learned a lot during my three years as a prison chaplain. I learned that many inmates have done absolutely horrendous things, and that a significant number are unable or unwilling to take responsibility for their actions. I also learned that prison is an incredibly hard place to become a better human being because of the violent and fearful nature of the surroundings. And I learned that the fence is pretty darn thin, and that with a slight change in genetic or environmental makeup or with a poor choice here or there, I could just as easily have been a resident in need of a chaplain rather than the one serving as a chaplain.

As a Catholic chaplain, I led weekly Word-Communion services on five yards (each yard functioned as a separate prison housing approximately 1,000 inmates) and once a month accompanied a bilingual priest who came to say Mass and hear confessions. I visited men in the prison hospital and in the "hole" (a prison within the prison for those who are caught selling drugs, fighting and so on). I comforted men who lost loved ones on the outside, and I taught a variety of classes on prayer and forgiveness and personal transformation. I lugged an artificial Christmas tree with me from yard to yard to brighten up our Advent and Christmas services and I led Stations of the Cross services during the season of Lent.

Though I had far more positive experiences with inmates than negative ones, I still found myself to be increasingly for the death penalty. In fact, when my family and I returned to the Twin Cities this past August, I was much more in favor of the death penalty—especially if the state had irrefutable DNA evidence—than against it. Why this shift in position?

Well, I had met quite a few inmates who had maimed and murdered and who didn't seem to be too concerned about their victims or victims' families. I read many prison files that contained narratives of their trials and disturbing pictures of their victims. It bothered me to see inmates with color televisions in their cells along with all sorts of snack food. I observed inmates happily playing volleyball, soccer, basketball, handball, softball, checkers, chess, dominos and cards, which some of their victims will never have a chance to do again. In short, it didn't seem fair or right that those who had intentionally taken another person's life should be able to enjoy things, much less live.

This was the mindset with which I returned to the Twin Cities. No, I wasn't bitter. I enjoyed my years as a chaplain. I met inmates who had changed for the better and inmates who were in the process of changing for the better. I knew inmates I would be happy to have as next-door neighbors and some I consider to be like brothers. I came to know many inmates who were wonderful, loving Catholics, who cared about those who were suffering in all corners of the world. Yet I came home in favor of the death penalty.

But then three things took place over the course of several months to change my stance on the death penalty so that I became more deeply against it than I was before I began my prison ministry.

First, I started to meditate again. I started to get out of my head, out of seeing things through my mind and limited ego, and started to get in touch with my heart. For as Antoine de Saint-Exupery so astutely observed, "It is only with the heart that one can see rightly." One purpose of prayer and meditation is to point out our blindness—which is inevitable when we rely solely on rational thought—and to restore our heart-sight, the vision with which Jesus saw and continues to see the world. If we Catholics don't pray and meditate, it becomes very easy to see life and complex issues such as capital punishment just the way others in our society do, through the understandable but distorted lens of "an eye for an eye" and "a life for a life." When we pray and meditate, the Holy Spirit gives us the eyes of Jesus, through which we can begin to see that the worst person among us has human dignity and potential for transformation. And that when we can't see this dignity and potential, God can.

Second, in conjunction with prayer and meditation, the words of the Gospel began to penetrate and break up the hardened regions of my heart, especially passages such as: "Love your enemies and pray for those who persecute you, so that you may be children of your Father in heaven; for he makes his sun rise on the evil and on the good, and sends rain on the righteous and on the unrighteous" (Mt 5:44–45).

Jesus' vision is that we are all one. Our brokenness keeps us from buying into this vision and living by this unalterable truth. And whatever happens to the least of us, to the victim and the murderer, happens not only to Jesus but to us all. Adding another victim through capital punishment does nothing to contribute to this oneness. Capital punishment is not only murder. It is killing someone who, like you and me, is made in the image of God. Our behavior does not change the fact that we are children of our Creator God and brothers and sisters of Jesus Christ.

Third, I was influenced by some reading I was doing on the stages of moral development. Generally speaking, many inmates are imprisoned within a childish developmental stage dominated by selfishness and an "everything centers around me" approach to life. If you want to punish inmates for murder, raise their morality, raise their consciousness, raise their humanity—don't kill them. Then as they develop as human beings, as they move up the moral ladder, so to speak, they will have true remorse and they will suffer for what they have done to hurt another human being. They will have to live with it. In fact, some transformed inmates will be aghast at what they did. I met at least 20 inmates during my three years who had metamorphosed from being heartless killers to tenderhearted human beings. They have an incredibly hard time forgiving themselves; in fact, many of them can't. They are trying to make a positive contribution, even though they may never see life again outside of prison. I am personally proud of these men and humbled that I had the privilege to come to know them.

It hurts for all of us to become more human, to open our minds and hearts and to have our circles of love expanded. The pain that murderers will suffer as they become more human is a pain that will hurt, but one that will also be redemptive. Jesus came to redeem the world and then passed the job along to us to continue ministering to the brokenness within and around us. When we say no to capital punishment, we are allowing the Spirit of relentless love to continue working in the hearts and minds of those we sometimes want to see pay with their lives. All we have to do is take an honest look at ourselves to see how much room there is for growth in our own journey to holiness and wholeness. And when we realize how far we have come and how far we have to go, we realize that we have no business saying that God cannot help a cold-blooded murderer become more human and holy in God's own way and time.

As the saying goes, "Be patient with me, for God isn't done with me yet." Our heads may say that the death penalty is fair; our Spirit-led hearts know that our God is out to heal all of us, whether we deem it fair or not.

The Mother of a Murderer Speaks Out Against the Death Penalty

Katherine Norgard

Katherine Norgard is a clinical psychologist who teaches and practices in Tucson. In the following article, she tells of the grief and despair she and her family suffered after her adopted son brutally murdered an elderly couple and was subsequently tried and sentenced to death. Norgard describes how saving his life took center stage and how she became obsessed with the death penalty. She shows too how her persistence paid off when a forensic discovery led to a new sentence of life for her son. Norgard details the grief and horror of her experience and reveals firsthand the impact of a death sentence on the family of the condemned.

The story I am about to tell began on August 29, 1989, at 2:00 A.M. when a telephone call interrupted my husband's and my sleep. That call and the events following it changed the rest of my life, propelling me into a state of chronic grief and despair.

My adopted son, John Eastlack, had been a constant heartache almost from the day we adopted him when he was a year and a half old. We got practically no information about his biological family since his records were sealed. That is how adoptions were conducted in 1969.

John was an affectionate child, athletic and musical, and brought joy into our small family. But he took things that did not belong to him. He did not learn easily at school or from his mistakes. He had trouble telling the truth. We tried every way we knew to help him—individual and family counselors, psychologists, tutors, and summer school. All I ever wanted was for John to grow up and be a happy, good citizen.

Everything we did failed to help. At fifteen, John was in a residential treatment center. Then the juvenile court sent him to a locked correctional facility when he was sixteen, and back again a second time where he stayed until he turned eighteen. Both times, the staff was puzzled as to why he was there. He was a star resident compared to the other boys, who were drowning in disadvantages.

At nineteen, John was put on adult probation. By twenty-one, he was in prison for using someone's credit card. . . .

That early morning phone call was from an official at the Department of Corrections. A male voice ordered us to open our front door. Two men from the fugitive division were waiting to talk to us.

They told us John and another young man had climbed the fence at Echo Unit, a minimum security prison on the outskirts of Tucson, between 7:30 and 9:30 P.M. the night before and had fled on foot across the desert toward town. Had we seen John? . . .

John had been transferred that week to Echo Unit from a prison in Florence, Arizona, where he had been in the "hole." He had been sent to Florence as a disciplinary measure for having a romantic relationship with a female guard at the Douglas prison, where he had been incarcerated. John's recent letters were different from his others. He talked nonsense saying that he was not really in prison, but was an FBI drug informant. It was as though he had snapped.

When we visited John that Saturday, he continued the crazy talk. "I have a car outside the fence. I can leave anytime I want," he said. We tried to help him get in touch with reality by pointing to the facts of his life. He could not hear us.

The second day John was on the run, he called home and spoke to Don while I was at work. "I'm in New Mexico. Everything's cool," John lied. Don urged John to turn himself in.

The evening television news featured John's photo, his prison number under his chin. He looked mean, not like the lovable person I knew who had never been violent or even in a fight. . . .

My daughter, Sonda, and her boyfriend, Jay, whom we were meeting for the first time, arrived from Colorado the day John escaped. I could not get my mind off John, but we pretended to have a normal family life in the midst of the unfolding drama.

Two days later, I still thought the authorities would apprehend John soon. He had always gotten caught in the past whenever he broke any rules. He had never been a successful criminal. Sonda asked Don to go to Colorado with her to help her winterize the biological lab buildings where she would be the winter caretaker. . . .

The day they left for Colorado, I wished I were with them when the temperature inside my old Toyota sports car was unbearable at four o'clock in the afternoon. They would be in the cool mountains by then. I climbed in to drive back to my office from the hospital where I consulted. . . .

A radio announcer's voice jarred into the capsule of my privacy. "John Patrick Eastlack, a convict who escaped from the Wilmot prison facility four days ago, is still at large. Eastlack has been charged with the murders of Leicester and Kay Sherrill. Sheriff's deputies found the elderly Sherrills bludgeoned to death at their east-side home. They were murdered sometime over the Labor Day weekend." . . .

The telephone rang as I entered my house. It was the first of an endless stream of reporters. . . .

The doorbell rang. Two men identified themselves as Tucson Police Department, Homicide. The larger one, who did most of the talking, asked if I was John Patrick Eastlack's mother. He said they had fingerprints and other evidence linking John to the Sherrill murders.

"Did he set fires as a kid? Was he cruel to animals? Has he ever used an alias?"

Never doubting their authority, I answered each question as any law-abiding citizen would. . . .

One of the nameless, faceless detectives asked, "Can we tap your telephone? Otherwise, we'll get a court order."

I nodded my consent. Today I wonder if my phone is still tapped.

As they left, one officer said, "This guy's a real creep. He's a serial killer." . . .

Television and newspaper reporters called all evening. The Tucson community was gripped by fear. Police had set up command posts in the area of the Sherrills' home. Fear brings out the best and the worst in people. Friends called and some crowded into our living room trying to support me and deal with their own shock. They answered the unending phone calls and kept reporters at bay. . . .

The next morning, I caught a flight to Colorado, counting on the police officers' promise to call me when they picked up John. . . .

Colorado offered no sanctuary.

Three days later, my friend Cindy Zahn called to tell me the police had picked John up in El Paso, Texas. She said John had confessed. . . .

The police never called. I was not given the ordinary respect they had promised. I had been betrayed. It was the first of many times to come that I felt treated like a criminal myself. . . .

Two weeks after we came home, I mustered enough courage to visit John. My hesitancy was not about John and his choices. I was petrified that I would encounter a reporter at the jail, because John was regularly giving them interviews. I did not want to be connected with any of the sensationalism. Throughout the whole ordeal, I never granted an interview to the media.

During that first visit, John said, "I really messed up this time, Mom. How could I have done such a terrible thing? There must be something wrong with my brain." I did not know then that the authorities could have been recording our conversation as John recounted details of his time in the Sherrills' house.

For years afterwards, every time I visited, John talked about the crime over and over. He used me as a priest, and I had no power to absolve him. I couldn't even stomach what I heard. He did the same with Don and with Sonda. Listening retraumatized me. It stirred up my own insanity over having failed at the most important job in the world—parenting my child. . . .

On September 20, 1989, I opened the newspaper to read John's confession letter to the presiding judge. Part of his letter stated: "I also want to make clear to you my reasons for going to the media as I did. Not because I want attention or to be a prison martyr. But to reassure my family and friends that what happened was indeed unexplainable and that I am not to be feared as the situation was before my capture. I am the person that was and still is their friend or family member."

On November 7, 1989, the headline told me that the state was seeking the death penalty. It was surreal. How could my government kill my son? . . .

On December 13, 1989, a newspaper article announced that John's public defender had withdrawn from his case over "fundamental differences." One of the lawyers called me and said that client-lawyer privilege prevented him from telling me any more. All I could ever imagine was that John went against their advice when he continued to call the media. . . .

Judge William Scholl appointed Ed Nesbitt, a contract attorney, to defend John. I wondered whether Ed, an African American, might understand John in some unique way, since John is part black and grew up in a white family.

I liked Ed as a person, but I had no way to evaluate his competence as a lawyer. He told me he had been a prosecutor and knew how prosecutors think. I arranged for periodic meetings with him to keep abreast of his plans. I always asked a friend, Don, or Sonda (who had moved back to Tucson to be present for John's trial) to attend and take notes.

My memory and thinking were impaired by the heavy fog of unrelenting grief. John begged me to get what he called a "brain test." Many times, I asked Ed to get John evaluated by a neuropsychologist or psychiatrist because the violent crime was so out of character for him. Ed repeatedly responded that John would be spending the rest of his life in prison and it was in John's best interest to be viewed there as "evil" rather than "sick." Persistence, one of my strong suits, got me nowhere with Ed.

Over and over, Ed told me, "It doesn't matter what I do or you do. John is going to be sentenced to death."

John did the crime. I never thought he was innocent. But he will always be my son. I could not imagine living if John got a death sentence and was executed. During other rough times in my life, I never considered suicide. Now, work was my only buffer from the hopelessness that had robbed me of my birthright of peace, love, and joy. I could not work every moment.

I could not sleep and had terrible nightmares. One persistent, repeated nightmare that robbed my sleep was that John and I were walking in our neighborhood and he said he wanted to go visit someone. He was too big for me to stop, and I could not keep up with him. I ran and ran and never found him again.

My gut ached constantly. I cried all the time. Alone in the world, I could no longer live with myself. I concocted a foolproof plan, which would look like an accident to everyone. . . .

Sonda's sad face flashed before me the day I had set to carry out my plan. She would have to live through it all. Some small patch of sanity stopped me. I had to go on living, if only for her sake. . . .

The clock moved forward. On November 1, 1990, jury selection for John's murder trial began. . . .

Ed said he was going to use self-defense as John's defense. Mr. Sherrill weighed 134 pounds and was in poor health. Mrs. Sherrill weighed about 90 pounds. John was a muscular 210 pounds and twenty-one years old! . . .

The second day of jury selection, we learned that John's jury had to be "death qualified." If a potential juror opposed the death penalty, even though the judge would be sentencing John, the person was automatically disqualified. Things were already stacking up against John. . . .

After the trial began on November 7, I called Ed again to find out the status of the neurological examination. He asked me to come up with the questions for the examiner and to recommend someone to perform it.

For three days, the prosecution presented witnesses and Ed cross-examined each one. Claire said John, dressed in his blazer and button-down shirt, swirled around in his chair looking like a college student rather than a criminal. . . .

The fourth day of trial, Claire called me at work. "Kathy, the pathologist testified. Don left, but Sonda sat through it all. It was brutal. All I could do was hold her hand. I'm worried about her."

I left work early. Sonda was lying on her bed, face down, her body shaking. "It's just too much, Mom," she said. "He's my brother. How could he do such a horrible thing?"

Ed called saying he was not going to put me on the stand after all. It was okay to come to court. The only witness Ed called to the stand was John, the self-admitted liar.

November 15, my haggard-looking face held my eyes in place with dark circles as I rode the elevator to the sixth floor of the courthouse. The only other person in the elevator with the three of us was [the prosecutor] Tom Zawada. He looked at the floor, never speaking or making eye contact. What was there to say? He was doing his best to make sure John would be killed. . . .

John was already in the courtroom. He turned around, giving me the same inappropriate grin he had used all his life. A smile struggled to lift the corner of my mouth. The television camera swung around to focus on me. . . .

Ed asked John why he had written a confession to the presiding judge. John explained that his emotions changed constantly, swinging from high to low, while he was in isolation at the jail. John said he "factually accepted that he had murdered the Sherrills," even though he said he would mentally never be able to accept that he did. Ed's last question to John was "Did you kill Mr. and Mrs. Sherrill? Did you cause their deaths?"

John answered, "Yes."

My shoulders touched my ears and my head ached.

Tom Zawada began cross-examining that same afternoon and continued into the next day. Zawada verbally badgered and mocked John.

Ed's only redirect questioning was to ask John if he had ever had a trial before or testified in front of a jury. John said, "No." The judge ended the day telling everyone to have a nice weekend. Court would reconvene the next week on Tuesday for jury instructions and closing arguments.

November 20, Zawada pranced around the courtroom holding the fireplace poker, telling the jury that John had poked, mashed, and bashed the Sherrills to death. He reminded the jury that John had called the Douglas prison to talk to an incarcerated friend there and told him he was having a "good time, the best days of his life."

Ed began his closing statement by saying that John bore responsibility for the deaths of two people, but he did not murder them. He pointed out that John had not planned anything, from the escape to the burning of the house he broke into. "A thinking person would have said, 'Oh well, I better not set this place on fire, because there will be smoke and fire people are going to show up.'"

Ed said that John was not a violent person, but that he went into a rage when he was in the Sherrills' house. "John is a liar. You can tell when John is lying. His lips are moving." He explained that John loved all the media attention because he had always been a nobody and the media made him famous. He said John told the reporters what they wanted to hear so they would keep coming back. "I only ask that the final headline be the truth . . . not what everybody wants to hear," Ed concluded.

The evening newspaper featured a photograph of John laughing in the courtroom. The caption said he smiled throughout his testimony.

Zawada capitalized on the photo the next day, calling John "Joking John Eastlack." He reminded the jury that John bashed, poked, and beat the Sherrills to death. I could not listen.

Judge Scholl had promised the jury they would be done before Thanksgiving. And they were. John waived his right to be present at the verdict since he did not like waiting in the small cage in the courtroom basement. I went to work. Ed said he would call me to come down for the verdict. Instead, a few hours later, Ed called saying the jury had found John guilty of two counts of felony murder and all the other charges of escape, arson, and burglary.

I had not had a full night's sleep for over fourteen months. Now my worst nightmare was official.

The next day was Thanksgiving. That morning's headline read, "Happy Thanksgiving," in red lettering. Underneath, in black print, it said, "Eastlack Guilty: May Get Death Penalty." We spent Thanksgiving alone, in shock.

John Hanna, a lawyer who worked for the Capital Representation Project, an agency that provides resources to capital defense lawyers, called me after the verdict. I had asked Ed to work with them, but Ed did not think it was necessary. Ed said he was setting things up for John's appeal. Hanna told me it is very difficult to overturn a death sentence on appeal. He urged me to hire an attorney to represent John at the sentencing hearing.

I met with several criminal attorneys and finally hired Carla Ryan, who specializes in death penalty cases. "Kathy, you have to do everything you can to prevent a death sentence. And in the process, you've got to press Nesbitt to present every possible mitigating factor so there will be a record when this thing goes to the Supreme Court on appeal," Carla said.

At our first meeting, I had no idea how dependent I, an ultra-independent person, would become on Carla over the next years. She came the next time I met with Ed.

Afterwards, Carla said we needed to get on record that Ed had said that nothing would prevent John being sentenced to death and that Ed himself was a "gambling buddy" of Judge Scholl. Carla said we should get affidavits for everyone who attended the meetings with Ed to get the judge's attention and put the facts into the record.

When Ed read the affidavits the next day at the sentencing hearing, April 2, 1991, he asked the judge to remove him from the case. He was worried that our family had poisoned his relationship with John. After all our efforts, the judge prevented Carla from presenting anything in court. . . .

I asked Ed to put me on the stand. Ann Nichols also agreed to testify. I had written out a lengthy statement for Ed elaborating the need for a neurological evaluation, my questions about attachment issues, genetic impact, and John's childhood history, and my feelings about him. I asked Ed to question me about these things on the stand.

My voice stuck in my throat when I spoke. Ed asked me the questions I had written for him. Trying to offset the image of "joking John Eastlack," I explained to the judge that John had always smiled inappropriately since we first got him when he was a year and a half old. Carla told me that the judge could find anything as a mitigating factor. I asked Judge Scholl to consider our family as mitigation since his sentence would affect my family and me forever. "Even behind bars, I believe John has something to contribute to society," I said. The judge looked at his yellow legal pad throughout my testimony and never once made eye contact. . . .

That evening's newspaper headline read "Eastlack's Mom Begs for His Life." We were now publicly connected.

Ann testified that she had known John since he was three years old and visited him while he was being held in the county jail. Ed established that Ann has a doctorate in social work. She told the judge that John was immature and functioned more like a thirteen-year-old than a twenty-three-year-old.

Ann's and my statements were the only mitigation Ed presented. Scholl set the sentencing for April 11, 1991.

The television crew was outside the courtroom when we arrived for the sentencing. The courtroom was packed. . . .

Without ever looking up from his legal pad, the judge stated that he had found two aggravating factors and no mitigating ones.

Frozen in my seat, I knew what was coming. I swallowed back tears as the television camera swung around to focus on the three of us.

". . . it is the judgment and sentence of the court that as to Count Seven, first-degree murder of Leicester Sherrill, that the defendant be sentenced to death. And as to Count Eight, the first-degree murder of Kathryn Sherrill, that the defendant be sentenced to death." . . .

We drove home, beyond tears. Friends arrived. The three of us sat together on our living room sofa like emigrants at the dock waiting for a ship to some foreign land. We no longer belonged in our lives.

Saving John's life became my focus. I searched out his birth mother and discovered that she had been a heavy drinker during her pregnancy with John. I tracked down people on both sides of his family and found a trail of mental illness, prostitution, drug addiction, suicide, and incarceration in their backgrounds. I made a trip to the Midwest to meet them. I also knew by then that avoiding or vacating a death sentence has more to do with the skill of the defense attorney than with mere facts.

Grief clouded my vision. I did not go through "stages" of grieving. Grief, or despair of this type, is a compound kind of suffering. I would be required to reinvent myself with the probability that John would be executed and the reality that he would never be in my physical life again. I had no road map for guidance. I floundered and faltered at every step. It was bad if people asked about John, but agonizingly terrible if they did not. He had become an invisible, nonexistent member of my family while still very much alive. . . .

Grief and despair were the price I paid for loving John. I kept telling myself that this whole experience needed to count for something. I wanted to help others. Gathering friends and colleagues together, I founded a nonprofit organization to end Arizona's death penalty. I served on the Arizona Civil Liberties Union board of directors and on the National Coalition to Abolish the Death Penalty. I began giving speeches and sermons and writing articles about abolition of the death penalty in Arizona and other parts of the country.

Colleagues urged me to "let go" and get on with life. One psychiatrist friend warned me that becoming an activist would ruin my psychotherapy practice. John was no longer just my son; he had become the centerpiece in my life. We were enmeshed. My recurring nightmare was both of us in his cell awaiting the executioner's footsteps coming down the hallway. Becoming an activist to end the death penalty, along with spiritual guidance and support from Marguerite Reed, improved my self-esteem and increased my trust in the world. Visiting death row regularly became a part of my routine, but it never felt normal.

I met other family members of the condemned. Each of them grappled with the same despair that had taken over my life. One mother committed suicide. Other families moved away, hoping geography would help them forget. Some contributed money for our abolition work, but none ever personally engaged in the work to end the death penalty to save their child. . . .

Kathleen DuBois and Robb Holmes, two dedicated Pima County Legal Defender attorneys, were assigned to represent John for his Arizona Supreme Court automatic appeal.

"For some reason, they have John on a fast track," Kathleen told me. "Normally, appeals do not come about this quickly." December 2, 1993, everyone, except John, was in court again to hear oral arguments on his appeal. . . .

John was a "paper person" to Colleen French who represented the attorney general's office. She had never even seen him. It was her first time arguing in front of this court, and her mother had come to watch. If Colleen French's mouth had been foaming, it would have matched her rabid appeal to uphold John's death sentence. John's attorneys, Kathleen and Robb, had worked hard and represented him well.

Waiting, hanging in limbo, was now commonplace in my life. Each day, I expected the phone call that eventually came on November 3, 1994. Robb announced that John's death sentence had been vacated and Judge Scholl was ordered to conduct a resentencing hearing. . . .

Sonda and Don had no faith Judge Scholl would change his sentence. This ray of hope was my answered prayer. The stark reality was that John's case could bounce around in the courts for years, and we would bounce with it. Life and death sentences seemed no different when I first accepted that John had killed Mr. and Mrs. Sherrill. Either way, he would die in prison. I realized over time that a life sentence is just that—life. A death sentence is murder by another name. After a person has been executed, the cause of death listed on the death certificate is "homicide." . . .

During the next years, I cannot say that I was responding to a spiritual call. I was obsessed. Carla and I were a great match. Like mine, her whole life centered around the death penalty.

Every waking moment, I planned and plotted how to get Carla Ryan to represent John. Accomplishing that through manipulation and sheer good luck, I devoured information about fetal alcohol syndrome, since John's birth mother drank to the point of blacking out while she was carrying John. I explored the issues of genetics, brain functioning, growing up in multiple foster homes, bonding and attachment, the impact of a divorce, and being in a stepfamily. I had ongoing contact with the postadoption social worker at the adoption agency to elicit her help in gaining information about John's past. I could leave no stone unturned to preserve his life.

Don's heart disease was not cured by the open heart surgery he had in 1990. He had problems with his hips and back related to a helicopter crash he had had in Viet Nam. Most disturbing to me was that he was caught in depression's web.

Sonda met and married Kevin Donovan in 1996.

I was only partially present for either Don or Sonda. Although I loved them both, my primary focus was always John. Saving his life was center stage for me. . . .

On February 25, 1997, almost eight years after John's crime, sixty friends and death penalty abolitionists packed the courtroom to standing room only to support our family and hear opening arguments at the resentencing trial. Judge John

Lindberg replaced Judge Scholl, who had been convicted of tax fraud related to gambling problems and removed from the bench. . . .

Tom Zawada, the original prosecutor, had been reprimanded for unethical conduct since John's original trial—I vaguely remember something in the newspaper about not following the professional rules required of prosecutors—but he was back on the case, dressed in his familiar dark suit, rambling on and on in his opening remarks about how John had killed the Sherrills. . . .

Carla started with Thomas Thompson, a neuropsychologist who had spent over thirty hours evaluating John and meeting with us and others John had known, and hundreds of hours reviewing the trial transcripts. Dr. Thompson, rarely smiling, presented a scholarly demeanor. He questioned whether John had "attachability," given that one of the sets of foster parents had given him back so they could go on vacation. "You tend not to give people back that you are attached to," Dr. Thompson testified. My mind wandered to Robie, my first husband, who had died just two years before, still denying any connection to John. . . .

Chris Cunniff, a pediatrician and geneticist, walked directly up to John and shook his hand before the startled armed guards swung into action to push him away. No one had touched John since 1991, not even me. Dr. Cunniff courageously broke all the rules. He testified about fetal alcohol syndrome and told the court John had the characteristic facial features (ptosis, epicanthic folds, depressed nasal bridge, a smooth philtrum, and a smooth upper lip) as evidenced in his infancy photos. Those features, coupled with his mother's alcohol history, indicated that John had a permanent fetal alcohol syndrome (FAS) disability. He said: "People with FAS don't learn to concentrate and remain on task. . . . They are impulsive; they do things without thinking. They don't understand consequences. They have an increased degree of petty criminality." He elaborated that even in an optimum rearing environment, behavior, learning, and development do not change significantly. People with FAS are immature and friendly and do not pick up on social cues. . . .

Carla's team had created a large genogram showing the family trees of John's birth families and his adoptive family. They used colors to represent mental disorders, alcoholism, drug addiction, and other problems various individuals had, and the trail all led to John. Carla established that substance abuse, behavioral disorders, institutionalizations, and affective disorders could be traced back five generations in John's birth family. When Carla put Dr. Thompson back on the stand, he said:

"If Mr. Eastlack had grown up in his biological family and had some of the types of problems he experienced, people would not be too surprised and many would say, 'Oh well, if we could just change the environment.' Well, the environment was changed." He explained that our family has a lot of strengths, but not enough to overcome the genetics, disruptions in attachment, and John's prenatal exposure to alcohol.

Dr. Thompson told the court that John's pervasive developmental disorder means that his central nervous system is not equipped to process the things necessary to succeed in his various roles in life. He explained that John's tendency to exaggerate and tell lies is common for people with pervasive developmental disorders: "People who can't adapt or fit in begin to become sealed off in their own world and begin to fabricate." Dr. Thompson explained that John cannot mediate between what he feels and what he does, he cannot think before he acts, and he does not learn from experience. . . .

Carla's last question—asking Dr. Thompson to explain what happened when John was in the Sherrills' house—brought a hush to the courtroom. Dr. Thompson said John was under the most stress he had ever experienced in his entire life. He was totally without external structure and was captured by the emotional reaction of the moment. His executive functioning was not sufficient to modify his emotions. Given that John had no history of violence, Dr. Thompson explained, "I think what you have here is an individual whose cognitive system is simply not able to deal with the emergence of the affect that occurred on that day."

Zawada began his rapid-fire cross-examination, jumping from subject to subject, as he did throughout the hearing. When he asked about the escape, Dr. Thompson explained it was still another example of a poorly thought out plan. He said that John is a poor con artist, and when he tries to put on different identities, it is almost ludicrous.

Carla showed two videotapes of interviews of longtime family friends, Joyce Lichtenstein and Sonia Maxwell. Both corroborated John's childhood difficulties, as did Don's, Sonda's, and my testimony. . . .

Two of my friends, Barbara Asmussen and Rosalie Barsky, testified that I had been a good mother. I slumped in my seat when Rosalie told the judge she had driven to the prison with me because I told her that was the only time I had to spend with our friends. Saving John's life was taking every waking moment of my life. . . .

When Sonda took the stand, she sounded relaxed and confident, as if she testified every day. She talked about feeling unsafe in the world after John killed the Sherrills. If her brother could do such an incomprehensible thing, how could she trust anyone else? . . .

Sonda . . . explained that she is a strong person, but John's death sentence had taxed her to the edge. All she could do was go to work and come home and be immersed in her sadness. "Having my brother on death row has changed what is relevant in the world. Not very many things seem important anymore." . . .

[On the stand] Don explained he had taken it for granted that John could learn. Don concluded by saying, "I've lost three grandchildren to birth defects. I didn't know about John's defects when he was growing up. I am pleading for you not to take John's life."

Zawada said, "This is pitiful. I couldn't cross-examine this man at this time."

Carla questioned me for several hours, establishing that John had never been violent, how we had tried to help him with the stealing problem, and our frustration with his learning problems. She also asked me how the death penalty had affected my life.

During cross-examination, Zawada asked me, "And you know if your body has a cancer or a tumor, you have to do something to remove it to protect the rest of your body." I heard a collective gasp from the audience. I felt my face flush with anger at the implication that John should be exterminated, just as Hitler had reasoned when he killed millions of Jews. Then I remembered some training about testifying as an expert witness and asked him to repeat the question. I said, "I am not sure what you are asking me."

"I have nothing further, Your Honor," Zawada said as he sat down. Again, we waited. This time we had full knowledge of how capricious the justice system is and there were no guarantees that John would get a better sentence.

On April 11, 1997, six years to the day after John had originally been sentenced to death, he looked handsome in his prison blue denim shirt and jeans as he stood between Carla and the other attorneys. Unlike at the first trial, when he had harmed himself with his comments, John responded, "No, sir," when the judge asked if he wanted to say anything before he was sentenced. Carla had coached him well.

Judge Lindberg began by saying he upheld the two aggravating factors. The first was that he had killed two people, and the second was that the murders were cruel and heinous.

I had been holding my breath. The courtroom was packed with our friends and supporters, some even sitting on the floor or standing around the edges of the room. Resuming my breathing, I heard Judge Lindberg list two mitigating factors— John's significant impairment and his age. It was two to two. Lindberg continued and began listing nonstatutory mitigators. First, he cited John's genetic history. Tears ran down my face. The judge was sentencing John to life! He listed six more nonstatutory factors (fetal alcohol syndrome, a limited ability to comprehend cause and effect, impaired judgment, a lack of control over behavioral responses, an ability to function in a structured environment, and a nonviolent history). There was a stir in the courtroom as Judge Lindberg sentenced John to two life sentences. The judge left the courtroom, and people in the audience hugged one another joyously.

Thankfully, I will never have to know how it would be if John were executed. During the year, as I have continued my fight to end the death penalty, I have met people whose loved ones were executed. Looking into their eyes, I have seen the familiar despair and inability to connect with the world around them. We create a new category of victims with the death penalty, the family of the condemned.

A Death Row Inmate Reflects on the Justice System and His Time on Death Row

Amy Goodman and Stanley "Tookie" Williams

Amy Goodman is an investigative journalist and host of Pacifica Radio's Democracy Now! *program. Stanley "Tookie" Williams was the founder of the Crips street gang who became well known as an anti-gang crusader while on death row. He was executed on December 13, 2005. In the following interview, which took place just two weeks before his execution, Williams insists on his innocence and describes the system that wrongly convicted him and sentenced him to death. He also talks about his time in prison, his "redemptive transition," his regrets, and his thoughts on the death penalty.*

In a half-hour interview, death row prisoner Stanley Tookie Williams speaks from his cell in San Quentin about his case, his life and his redemption. He helped start the Crips street gang—his greatest regret—but behind bars he has become a leading advocate for the end of gang violence. He has written nine books and has been nominated several times for the Nobel Peace Prize. He is scheduled to die on Dec. 13, [2005] unless, [California] Governor [Arnold] Schwarzenegger grants him clemency. Actions are planned across the world today in what has been described as International Save Tookie Day.

AMY GOODMAN: Hello? Stanley Williams?

STANLEY TOOKIE WILLIAMS: Yes, it is.

Thank you for joining us. I know you don't have much time, so I want to ask why you are petitioning the governor for executive clemency?

Amy Goodman and Stanley "Tookie" Williams, "A Conversation with Death Row Prisoner Stanley Tookie Williams from His San Quentin Cell," *Democracy Now!*, www.democracynow.org, November 30, 2005. Reproduced by permission.

I'm petitioning—my attorneys are petitioning the governor because I am innocent, but primarily, they're trying to save my life so that, inevitably, I will be able to prove my innocence.

Can you talk about the crime that you were convicted of? Are you guilty of that crime?

No, I am not culpable of those crimes. I have been stating that fact from the incipient, from the moment of my arrest. False arrest.

Why do you think the jury found you guilty?

Oh, it was quite easy. It was a paradigm of racism. We are talking about prosecutorial misconduct. We are talking about exclusion of exculpatory evidence. We are talking about I.A.C., which is ineffective assistance of counsel. We are talking about biased jury selection, which results in an all-white jury. We're talking about involuntary psychotherapic druggings, the misuse of jailhouse and government informants. And last, but not least not a shred of tangible evidence, no fingerprints, no crime scenes of bloody boot prints. They didn't match my boots, nor eyewitnesses. Even the shotgun shells found conveniently at each crime scene didn't match the shotgun shells that I owned.

Were you there that night?

STANLEY TOOKIE WILLIAMS: No, I wasn't. Everything was predicated on hearsay and circumstantial evidence.

Why do you believe the police arrested you?

STANLEY TOOKIE WILLIAMS: Because of my past. Because of my history. I was the co-founder of the Crips. I was someone that, whenever anything happened pretty much in L.A. [Los Angeles] or in Compton, for instance—as an example, in Compton, the Compton armory had been broken into and quite a few weapons were missing. Of course, they automatically assumed that I had something to do with it or I knew of someone who broke in there, and I was submitted—I had to—I was subjected to two lie detector tests.

And yet they still arrested you?

Oh, yes. Oh, yes. I have been picked up for many strange cases. Some—I even had Johnnie Cochran to represent me for a attempted robbery on two individuals who, in a sense, were broker than I was; they were more destitute than I was, but yet, still, I attempted to rob them. . . .

Stanley Williams, can you describe where we're talking to you right now?

STANLEY TOOKIE WILLIAMS: Well, I am on San Quentin's death row. I'm in a cell that's probably nine by four or nine by five feet—or foot, rather. And there's a steel sink. There's a steel toilet. There's a steel bunk. There's a steel shelf. There's a light fixture. And on the bars is—on the outside of the bars is a mesh fence. . . .

Can you talk about your time there? Can you talk about the beginning, the years in solitary confinement and what you've done?

Well, I can quite—I can easily demythologize the thought that, well, a person, when he goes to prison, of course, they'll change. They're locked up. That's not so, because I was incorrigible from the moment I got here all the way up to 1988, so that debunks that theory. And once I was in solitary confinement, it provided me with the isolated moments to reflect on my past and to dwell upon something greater, something better than involving myself in thuggery and criminality. It had to be more to life than that. It had to be more than the madness that was disseminating throughout this entire prison.

And so, when do you feel like you started to change?

Between the years of 1988 to 1994, and it's a continuous—it's an incessant reality for me. My redemptive transition began in solitary confinement, and unlike other people who express their experiences of an epiphany or a satori, I never experienced anything of that ilk. Mine—that wouldn't have been enough. I often tell people that I didn't have a 360-degree turnaround; I had a 720-degree turnaround. It took me twice as much. Just one spin around wouldn't have done it. I was that messed up, that lost, that mentacided, brainwashed. So, I was able to gradually in a piecemeal fashion change my life slowly but surely through education, through edification, through spiritual cultivation, battling my demons. And eventually, that led to me embracing redemption.

And what does embracing redemption mean? Can you talk about your writing? Can you talk about what you have done?

Well, my interpretation of redemption, it differs from the theological or the academical rendition. I believe that my redemption symbolizes the end of a bad beginning and a new start. It goes beyond, in a sense of being liberated from one's sins or atonement in itself. I feel that my redemption mostly or primarily encompasses the ability to reach out to others. I call it—when people say spirituality, I break it down as a spirit act, with "spirit" being the [inaudible] of the soul, the id, etc., etc., and the "uality" aspect of it being an act, a performance, a deed. So, we're talking about a spirit act, a spirit act towards helping other people, which are primarily youths in my case.

And what is the message that you are trying to send? Who are you talking to among the youth in this country?

I'm talking to any youth who are considered to be or deemed to be at-risk or even hinting around being a thug or a criminal of any type of genre. I mostly propagate education and the need for it, because to me, that is the terra firma in which any human being must stand in order to survive in this country or to survive anywhere in the world, in dealing, you know, with every aspect of civilization, every aspect of surviving. Education is very important. It took me all of these years to discern that, and now I do.

Stanley Williams, can you talk about why you started the Crips?

Well, I mean, I stated it in my memoir, *Blue Rage, Black Redemption*, that we started out—at least my intent was to, in a sense, address all of the so-called neighboring gangs in the area and to put, in a sense—I thought I can cleanse the neighborhood of all these, you know, marauding gangs. But I was totally wrong. And eventually, we morphed into the monster we were addressing.

In what way?

Well, we became a gang. We became exactly what I had odium for, which were gangs, street gangs. I mean, there were—they became a pest. They were a pest. Every time I looked up, my friends were being preyed upon. And when I came from camp, I decided to create something that would deal with them, to put them in their place. I mean, it's—it's really ironic, because we did too good of a job, and we morphed into what we were fighting, what we were battling against.

Stanley Williams, your critics say you might be running the Crips from death row. What is your response to that?

Well, I say that whomever says that, whatever institution or singular person says that, that you must take that and society must take that with a grain of salt. I say that, because of the simple fact that I have documentation in which—if you know my editors of the books, of my children's books, Ms. Barbara Becnel, she can forward you or email you the chronicles that I received from the Institutional Classification Committee that commended me on my positive program over the last ten years, and that's dated on August 5, 2004. So, that in a sense contradicts anything that anyone is saying. This— what they're saying, these lies, these spurious allegations that these people are throwing out there are just something that they're putting out there in order to exacerbate, to expedite my execution. I mean, any time that they can make it appear as though I'm still a monster, then society will say, "Well, kill him." It facilitates my death. Common sense. That's what it does. That's what these people have been trying to do for the last five years with impetus. This is what they have been doing.

Stanley Williams, what are you most proud of in your life?

Other than writing the children's books and my memoir, my redemption and my change. I never thought, ever, that I would be able to change because of the simple fact—Thuggery was all I knew. I lived it. I breathed it. Being a Crip was all I knew. I thought there was nothing else. I dreaded life after Cripping. I dreaded that. But I say to any individual who is in a gang that if you have enough courage to get into a gang, you should have equally enough or even more to get out of it. . . .

December 13 is just two weeks away from this conversation.

Yes, it is.

What are your thoughts facing your death?

I have none. In other words, I continue to live my life day by day, or shall I say, minute by minute, hour by hour, and day by day, as I have been doing since my redemption. It has nothing to do with a cavalier attitude. It has nothing to do with machismo or manhood or some pseudo code of the streets, which I formerly used. It has to do with my faith in God and my redemption. That's why I can sit here and talk to you just as calmly or any of the other journalists who have crossed my path. I don't fear this type of stuff, I'm at peace. . . . And when you maintain this sense of peace and you live by truth, by integrity, these things don't bother me. It doesn't. I have been experiencing moribund type experiences most of my life. I could have died many a times. I could have died when I was shot. I could have died when I was shot at by the police and rival gang members. There were many opportunities for me to die. Of course, I don't want to die. I mean, after my redemption I have what I consider to be a joie de vivre, so, you know, I have an enjoyment, a love for life. So that's why I can calmly sit here and speak to you or anyone else with peace in my heart and peace in my mind. I don't get rattled. Nothing can rattle me. Nothing will ever rattle me. I have been rattled the majority of my life.

I asked you what you are most proud of in your life. What do you most regret?

Creating the Crips. That is my—I rue that more than anything.

You managed to strike a peace accord. How did you maneuver that between the Crips and the Bloods?

Well, the fact that a person such as me, of my ilk, who deemed the opposing gang as an eternal enemy, it wasn't hard for people to believe me, because they knew where I stood. There were no clandestine or latent messages. Everybody knew where I stood. And for me to come out and say that what we were doing was wrong, it was believable. That's why people didn't—or at least the gang members didn't discredit my propensity and my alacrity for peace. That's why I was embraced with sincerity by those who I knew and those I didn't know on both sides of the fence.

Stanley Williams, what does it mean to have the level of support that you have right now?

It's God-inspiring to me, awe-inspiring. It's excellent. I'm exceptionally grateful. I never expected it. The majority of my life, I have fought, especially in here, alone. Even—I even had to fight against the attorneys, the incompetent attorneys, appeal attorneys, appellate attorneys, rather, that I had representing me, who were not qualified. I had one attorney who was an employment litigator, job litigator, you know, on the federal level, and she had been on that for like three years, and this woman was coming to represent me for four murders?

Then they had a guy that represented me. He only represented me for six months, because after that, he had to end up leaving and going to Ireland somewhere. Now, he knew prior to that that he had an engagement, but yet he took the case, allowing me to think that he was going to be permanent. He said he was going to be permanent. But yet, still, he left within six months. As a matter of fact, it was five-and-a-half months in which he left.

So, these are the things—these are the type of representations that I was getting, attorneys who would file a brief, a 27-page or 45-page brief with over 120 typos in it, and telling me that, 'Oh, well, you know, the judge wouldn't—it doesn't matter. They won't look at that.' Of course, they'll look at that. And they'll use that against me, not her, me.

What are your thoughts on the death penalty, in general?

The death penalty, it's not a system of justice, it is a system of—a so-called system of justice that perpetuates a, shall I say, a vindictive type of response, a vigilante type of aura upon it. We're talking about something that is barbaric. We're talking about something that—it doesn't deter anything. I mean, if it did, then it wouldn't be so many—especially in California, we're talking about over 650 individuals on death row. And if it was a deterrent, this place wouldn't be filled like this. And it's an expensive ordeal that—the money, as you know, the monetary means comes out of the taxpayers' pocket.

And for anyone to think that murder can be resolved by murdering, it's ridiculous. I mean, we look at all of the wars that we have throughout other countries and other nations, and all it does is—this violence, all it does is engender violence. There seems to be no end, but a continuous cycle, an incessant process of blood and gore that doesn't end. And through violence, you can't possibly obtain peace. You can, in a sense, occupy a belief of peace; in other words, through this mechanism of violence, you—it appears that because there is a standing army or standing police that is used in brutality or violence or a system that uses brutality or violence that that is going to totally eliminate or stop criminous behavior or criminous minds or killings or what have you, but it doesn't. . . .

Do you ever imagine yourself being free?

In my dreams. In my dreams I've envisioned my liberation many a times. As a matter of fact, I was telling an individual the other day that in my dreams, whenever I run into some albatross or some type of dilemma, I seem to float away from it. And in my mind, that is a sense of freedom. That is a sense of avoiding, eschewing or shunning any type of madness.

Do you know how the state plans to kill you?

Well, if I don't, I'd have to be living in a cave somewhere.

How will they do it?

Well, through, you know, the intravenous use of needles and things of that nature.

Are they preparing you for this now?

Preparing me?

Yes.

Well, yes. I'm in a different area. I used to be in East block, and now I'm in North 6. So, yes, yes, they are, of course. In their minds, it's a done deal.

And in your mind?

I'm sure they're looking forward to it, because they have come out propagating that I should be executed. Isn't that amazing? This is unprecedented for the C.D.C. [California Department of Correction] or San Quentin prison—and/or San Quentin prison to come out against an individual; it's never been done before in the history of this institution, or the history of C.D.C. But yet, they have come out.

Can you explain what you mean?

Well, I mean, they have—you find there are individuals they have, like for instance, the San Quentin spokesperson, he spoke out. He said—even on *60 Minutes*, they did a program about me, and he stated that I deserved to be executed. Now, I believe that's taking your job too far. And at one time, they had a lot of spurious allegations on the C.D.C. website, which they had to take off, because the former San Quentin warden. [Daniel B.] Vasquez, he stated that San Quentin appears to be trying to promote death by getting into this. They're supposed to be impartial. Their job is only to execute me, not to exacerbate by drumming up the need, the protests, or the remonstration for me to be executed, but that's what they have been doing, I'm the only human being that's ever been on death row that they have ever put forth effort to execute.

If the Governor—

Unprecedented.

If the Governor, if Governor Schwarzenegger, grants you executive clemency, what will you do? What are your plans? What do you want to do?

There's so many things. I'm glad—excellent question. I'm glad you asked that. The thing is, recently, I had a visit with Bruce Gordon. He is the President and C.E.O. of the NAACP. I had a visit with him on the 25th, Friday, and we have established a partnership to create a violence prevention curriculum for at-risk youth throughout America, and each of the chapters of NAACP are implementing this program. And he is going around the country promoting this and apprising people. So I'm not sitting back on my laurels, believe me. . . .

Do you think you could be granted a new trial?

Well, that's dealing in hypotheticals, and I don't deal with hypotheticals. I can only say that I pray that I get a new trial. I pray that I get whatever is necessary to spare my life, so that I can continue to strive in order to prove my innocence.

And if you still spent the rest of your life in jail, do you think it would be worth being spared the death penalty?

Oh, well, of course. I mean, where there's life, there's the ability to continuously strive to do whatever your purpose is or goal is in life. So, yes, if I'm alive, I can always strive forward to prove my innocence, regardless of how long it takes, even up to the last second of my life, and I'm 100 or whatever. . . . As I stated earlier in the conversation, that I have joie de vivre. So with this love of life, I have it. I assume that was forged down to me from my ancestors. So—

Well, in these last seconds that we have, they're yours. What do you have to say?

Well, I want to thank you for allowing me to be able to express my thoughts and feelings, and that as long as I have breath, I will continue to do what I can to proliferate a positive message throughout this country and abroad to youths everywhere, of all colors or gender and geographical area, and I will continue to do what I can to help. I want to be a part of the—you know, the solution. . . .

Organizations to Contact

The editors have compiled the following list of organizations concerned with the issues presented in this book. The descriptions are derived from materials provided by the organizations. All have publications or information available for interested readers. The list was compiled on the date of publication of the present volume; the information provided here may change. Be aware that many organizations take several weeks or longer to respond to inquiries, so allow as much time as possible.

American Civil Liberties Organization (ACLU)
Capital Punishment Project, Durham, NC   27701
(919) 682-5659
Web site: www.aclu.org

The Capital Punishment Project (CPP) is a national project of the American Civil Liberties Union. The CPP engages in public education and advocacy, systemic reform, and strategic litigation, including direct representation of capital defendants. The CPP challenges the unfairness and arbitrariness of capital punishment while working toward its ultimate repeal. It publishes and distributes numerous books and pamphlets, including *Mental Illness and the Death Penalty in the United States, How the Death Penalty Weakens U.S. International Interests,* and *Dead End: A No-Nonsense Resource on Capital Punishment.*

Amnesty International USA
Program to Abolish the Death Penalty, New York, NY   10001
(212) 807-8400 • fax: (212) 627-1451
Web site: www.amnestyusa.org/abolish

Amnesty International (AI) is a worldwide movement of people who campaign for internationally recognized human rights. Amnesty International USA's Program to Abolish the Death Penalty works for an end to executions and the cycle of violence created by a system riddled with economic and racial bias and tainted by human error. It publishes the reports *Encourage Worldwide Abolition, The Execution of Mentally Ill Offenders*, and numerous fact sheets on capital punishment.

Campaign to End the Death Penalty
PO Box 25730, Chicago, IL   60625
(773) 955-4841
Web site: www.nodeathpenalty.org

The Campaign to End the Death Penalty (CEDP) is the only national membership-driven, chapter-based grassroots organization dedicated to the abolition of capital punishment in the United States. With active chapters in cities and campuses across the country, the organization works with those who have experienced the horrors of death row firsthand—death row prisoners themselves their family members—to ensure that their voices are at the forefront of the abolitionist movement. Its semiannual newsletter, *The New Abolitionist*, is a forum for activists, death row prisoners, and others to discuss the issues and to raise questions and debates about how to end the death penalty.

Catholics Against Capital Punishment (CACP)
P.O. Box 5706, Bethesda, MD   20824-5706
fax: (301) 654-0925
Web site: www.cacp.org

Catholics Against Capital Punishment was founded in 1992 to promote greater awareness of Catholic Church teachings that characterize capital punishment as unnecessary, inappropriate and unacceptable in today's world. Its newsletter, *CACP News Notes*, disseminates news about Catholic-oriented anti–death penalty efforts.

Citizens United for Alternatives to the Death Penalty (CUADP)
2603 Dr. Martin Luther King Jr. Hwy, Gainesville, FL   32609
(800) 973-6548

Web site: www.cuadp.org

Citizens United for Alternatives to the Death Penalty (CUADP) works to end the death penalty in the United States through campaigns of public education and the promotion of tactical grassroots activism.

Clark County Indiana Prosecuting Attorney
Web site: www.clarkprosecutor.org/html/death/death.htm

Steven D. Stewart, prosecuting attorney for Clark County, Indiana, has established a Web site with information on Indiana's death penalty and an extensive listing of death penalty–related sites. Stewart argues that the death penalty is the appropriate punishment for society's worst crimes and claims that anti–death penalty advocates mislead the public about the number of innocent and exonerated prisoners on death row.

Death Penalty Focus
870 Market Street, Suite 859, San Francisco, CA   94102
(415) 243-0143 • fax: (415) 243-0994
Web site: www.deathpenalty.org

Founded in 1988, Death Penalty Focus is a nonprofit organization dedicated to the abolition of capital punishment through grassroots organizing, research, and the dissemination of information about the death penalty and its alternatives. It publishes and distributes a newsletter, *The Sentry*, which provides comprehensive information and editorials on the death penalty on a local, national, and international scale. It also publishes materials on the death penalty such as *Myths and Facts About the Death Penalty, The Catalyst News Bulletin, Fact Sheets on Youth and the Death Penalty, The Federal Death Penalty*, and *10 Reasons to Oppose the Death Penalty*.

Death Penalty Information (DPINFO)
Web site: www.dpinfo.com

The DPINFO offers the latest death penalty headlines, articles, and up-to-date pro-death penalty information. It includes articles and links to publications in support of capital punishment.

Death Penalty Information Center (DPIC)
1101 Vermont Avenue NW, Suite 701, Washington, DC   20005
(202) 289-2275 • fax: (202) 289-7336
Web site: www.deathpenaltyinfo.org

The Death Penalty Information Center is a nonprofit organization serving the media and the public with analysis and information on issues concerning capital punishment. Founded in 1990, the Center prepares in-depth reports, issues press releases, and conducts briefings for journalists and serves as a resource to those working on this issue. The Center is widely quoted and consulted by all those concerned with the death penalty. The organization's numerous publications, such as *Blind Justice: Juries Deciding Life and Death with Only Half the Truth, Innocence and the Crisis in the American Death Penalty*, and annual reports on the death penalty in the United States, are available on its Web site.

Justice for All
Web site: www.jfa.net

Justice for All is a Texas-based nonprofit organization advocating for criminal justice reform with an emphasis on victim rights. The organization is a strong advocate of the death penalty, and has established a separate site, Prodeathpenalty.com, dedicated to pro–death penalty information and resources. It has also established Murdervictims.com for survivors of victims of homicide.

The Lamp of Hope Project
P.O. Box 305, League City, TX   77574-0305

Established in 1991, the Lamp of Hope Project (LHP) is a nonprofit corporation primarily administered by death row prisoners that strives to shed light on the truth about the terrible conditions of the justice system. It seeks also to address victims' rights; the effects of poverty on crime; the concerns of the family members of the incarcerated, especially those on death row; the dignity and integrity of death row inmates; the improvement of the relationship between inmates and the outside community; and the protection of prisoners' interests and civil rights. It publishes prisoner writings and the *Death Row Journal*, which are available on its Web site.

The Mid-Atlantic Innocence Project (MAIP)
American University, Washington College of Law
Washington, DC   20016
(202) 274-4199 or (202) 274-4162 • fax: (202) 730-4733
Web site: www.exonerate.org

The Mid-Atlantic Innocence Project (MAIP) is a nonprofit organization that provides investigative and legal assistance to incarcerated people who have been wrongly convicted. MAIP, which was founded in 2000 as the Innocence Project of the National Capital Region, is run through a network of attorneys and law students throughout Virginia, Maryland, and the District of Columbia. Under the supervision of professors and local attorneys, students investigate claims of innocence from prisoners in cases involving DNA evidence or other newly discovered evidence of innocence. Pro bono attorneys then take over those cases in which the students have found a potentially demonstrable claim of innocence.

The Moratorium Campaign
586 Harding Blvd., Baton Rouge, LA   70807
Web site: www.moratoriumcampaign.org

The Moratorium Campaign, founded by Sister Helen Prejean, works to see every state declare a moratorium on executions. It aims to help people throughout the country take solid, practical steps toward achieving a moratorium in their state. Its Web site contains an online petition to end the death penalty and makes available Prejean's books, *Death of Innocents* and *Dead Man Walking*.

Murder Victims Families for Human Rights (MVFHR)
2161 Massachusetts Ave., Cambridge, MA   02140
(617) 491-9600

Web site: www.murdervictimsfamilies.org/

Murder Victims Families for Human Rights (MVFHR) is an organization with a national and international focus actively working to abolish the death penalty. MVFHR members are murder victims' family members and family members of the executed who are opposed to killing in all cases whether it be homicide, state killing, or extrajudicial killings and "disappearances." It publishes newsletters and annual reports on the death penalty, including *Creating More Victims: How Executions Hurt the Families Left Behind.*

Murder Victims Families for Reconciliation (MVFR)
2100 M St. NW, Suite 170-296, Washington, DC   20037
(877) 896-4702
Web site: www.mvfr.org

Based in Washington, D.C., MVFR is a national organization that relies on local volunteers to work with their communities, their neighbors, their local newspapers and local decision makers to tell the stories of murder victim family members and families of the executed who do not want the death penalty.

National Center for Policy Analysis Idea House: Capital Punishment
601 Pennsylvania Ave., Washington, DC   20004
(202) 220-3082 • fax: (202) 220-3096
Web site: www.ncpa.org

The National Center for Policy Analysis is a nonprofit think tank. Its section on crime and punishment includes a number of brief pro–death penalty articles from newspapers and other publications.

Prisonersolidarity.org
P.O. Box 422, The Plains, OH   45780

The Internet site *Prisonersolidarity.org* serves as a catalyst for communication between prisoners and people on "the outside." It publishes updated research, news, opinion pieces and educational material from activists, writers, prisoners, and the concerned public.

Pro-Death Penalty.com

Pro-Death Penalty.com is an online resource for pro–death penalty information. Includes a database of victims of death row inmates, responses to abolitionist arguments and articles, and links to essays and books in support of capital punishment.

Bibliography

Books

Elizabeth Beck, Sarah Britto, and Arlene Andrews — *In the Shadow of Death: Restorative Justice and Death Row Families.* Oxford: Oxford University Press, 2007.

Hugo Bedau and Paul Cassell, eds. — *Debating the Death Penalty: Should America Have Capital Punishment?* New York: Oxford University Press, 2004.

John Bessler — *Kiss of Death: America's Love Affair with the Death Penalty.* Boston: Northeastern University Press, 2003.

Joan Cheever — *Back from the Dead: One Woman's Search for the Men Who Walked Off America's Death Row.* Hoboken, NJ: John Wiley & Sons Inc., 2006.

Kerry Max Cook — *Chasing Justice.* New York: HarperCollins, 2007.

David Dow — *Executed on a Technicality: Lethal Injustice on America's Death Row.* Boston: Beacon, 2005.

Mike Ferrell — *Just Call Me Mike: A Journey to Actor and Activist.* New York: RDV Akashic, 2007.

Benjamin Fleury-Steiner — *Jurors' Stories of Death: How America's Death Penalty Invests in Inequality.* Ann Arbor: University of Michigan Press, 2004.

Stephen P.
Garvey, ed.

America's Death Penalty: Beyond Repair? Durham, NC: Duke University Press, 2003.

Craig Haney

Death by Design: Capital Punishment as a Social Psychological System. New York: Oxford University Press, 2005.

Norma Herrera

Last Words from Death Row: The Walls Unit. Mequon, WI: Nightengale, 2007.

Judith W. Kay

Murdering Myths: The Story Behind the Death Penalty. Lanham, MD: Rowman & Littlefield, 2005.

Helen Prejean

The Death of Innocents: An Eyewitness Account of Wrongful Executions. New York: Random House, 2004.

Matthew
Robinson

Death Nation: The Experts Explain American Capital Punishment. New York: Prentice-Hall, 2007.

Austin Sarat

When the State Kills: Capital Punishment and the American Condition. Princeton, NJ: Princeton University Press, 2002.

Susan Lee
Campbell Solar

No Justice: No Victory—The Death Penalty in Texas. Austin, TX: Plain View, 2004.

Scott Sundby

A Life and Death Decision: A Jury Weighs the Death Penalty. New York: Palgrave Macmillan, 2005.

Scott Turow	*Ultimate Punishment: A Lawyer's Reflections on Dealing with the Death Penalty.* New York: Farrar, Straus & Giroux, 2003.
Margaret Vandiver	*Lethal Punishment: Lynchings and Legal Executions in the South.* New Brunswick: Rutgers University Press, 2006.
Courtney Vaughn	*Living with the Death Penalty.* Courtney Vaughn/Xlibris Corporation, 2007.
Welsh S. White	*Litigating in the Shadow of Death: Defense Attorneys in Capital Cases.* Ann Arbor: University of Michigan Press, 2006.
Franklin E. Zimring	*The Contradictions of American Capital Punishment.* Oxford: Oxford University Press, 2003.

Periodicals

Rosalynn Carter	"No Death Penalty for Juveniles." *Miami Herald,* April 7, 2004.
Richard Cohen	"A Delusional System of Justice," *Washington Post,* December 26, 2006.
Hashem Dezhbakhsh and Joanna M. Shepherd	"The Deterrence Effect of Capital Punishment: Evidence from a 'Judicial Experiment.'" *Economic Enquiry* 44, no. 3, July 2006: pp. 512–35.

John Donohue and Justin J. Wolfers — "The Death Penalty: No Evidence for Deterrence" *The Economists Voice* 3, no. 5 (2006): Article 3.

Jennifer L. Eberhardt, Paul G. Davies, Valerie J. Purdie-Vaughns, and Sheri Lynn Johnson — "Looking Deathworthy: Perceived Stereotypicality of Black Defendants Predicts Capital-Sentencing Outcomes." *Psychological Science* 17, no. 5 (2006): pp. 383–86.

Denise Grady — "Doctors See Way to Cut Suffering in Executions." *New York Times,* June 23, 2006.

Frank Green — "Some Murder Victims' Kin Reject Capital Punishment; Others Endorse the Sanction." *Richmond Times-Dispatch,* December 22, 2003.

Orin Guidry — "Message From the President: Observations Regarding Lethal Injection," American Society of Anesthesiologists June 30, 2006.

Patrick D. Healy — "Death Penalty Seems Unlikely to Be Revived." *New York Times,* February 11, 2005.

Bob Herbert — "Who Gets the Death Penalty?" *New York Times,* May 13, 2002.

Harold Hongju Koh and Thomas R. Pickering — "American Diplomacy and the Death Penalty." *Foreign Service Journal,* October 2003: pp. 19–25.

Jeffrey M. Jones — "Americans' Views of Death Penalty More Positive This Year," *Gallup Poll News Service,* May 19, 2005.

Dan Levey "Balancing the Scales of Justice." *Judicature* 89, no. 5, March–April, 2006: pp. 289–91.

Richard Pompelio "For Survivor's Sake, Abolish the Death Penalty." *Star Ledger*, June 12, 2006.

Maurice Possley and Steve Mills "Did This Man Die. . . for This Man's Crime?" *Chicago Tribune*, June 25–27, 2006.

Austin Sarat "Schwarzenegger's Mistake: Clemency and Tookie Williams." *Jurist*, December 27, 2005.

James D. Unnever and Francis T. Cullen "The Racial Divide in Support for the Death Penalty: Does White Racism Matter?" *Social Forces* 85, no. 3, March 2007: 1281–1302.

Harry Weinstein and Maura Dolan "The Chaos Behind California Executions." *Los Angeles Times*, October 2, 2006.

Index

A

Abolitionist movement
  organizations in, 31
  strengthening of, 12–13,
  15–16
Abolitionists
  arguments of, 11–12, 43–44,
  119–123
  on immorality of death pen-
  alty, 49
Abu-Jamal, Mumia, 91–92
Aeropagus, 45
African Americans, death penalty
  and, 13–14, 77–78
Age issues, 113–117
Aggravating factors, 46, 50, 52, 63,
  93, 106, 146
Al Qaeda, 86, 87
Alito, Samuel, Jr., 62, 66
Allen, Clarence Ray, 114–117
Alley, Sedley, 64
American Bar Association (ABA),
  16, 28
Ancient Greece, 44–46
Anger, 54
Animal euthanasia, 59–60
Annan, Kofi, 16
Appellate review, 21, 27
Appellate rights, 98
Archer, Dane, 83
Aristotle, 53, 54
Atkins v. Virginia (2002), 17, 102,
  107

B

Babbitt, Bill, 95
Babbitt, Manny, 94–95
Beccaria, Cesare, 11–12

Bedau, Hugo Adam, 20
Bell, House v. (2006), 64
Bible, 11
Black, Charles, 87
Blackmun, Harry A., 25, 63, 105
Blecker, Robert, 43, 90, 99
Blood pollution, 45, 46
"Blood price," 44–45
Bowman, Kathleen, 38–39
Brauchli, Christopher, 57
Breyer, Stephen, 62–63
Brown, California v. (1987), 54
Brown v. Saunders (2006), 64
Bruck, David, 63
Brutalization effect, 12
Bush, George W., 23, 29

C

California, 82
California v. Brown (1987), 54
Callins v. Collins (1994), 63
Capital cases
  appellate review in, 21, 27
  errors in, 62
  judicial scrutiny in, 70–71
  role of juries in, 105–108
  sentencing errors in, 89–99
Capital jurisprudence, 52–53
Capital Jury Project, 24–25
Capital punishment. *See* Death
  penalty
Capital Representation Project,
  138
Catholicism, 126–127
Clinton, Bill, 16
Closure, 30–31

Coe, Robert, 96–97

Coleman, Roger Keith, 68, 72

Collins, Callins v. (1994), 63

Commutations of sentences, 21–22

Constitution Project, 63

Convictions, erroneous, 14–15, 26, 63–64, 89–90

Crips, 151–153, 154

Crow Dog, 39

Cruel and unusual punishment
    death penalty as, 13, 25, 32, 52
    evolving standard of, 49
    juvenile executions as, 100–101

Cruz, Rolando, 14

Culpability, 110–111

Cunniff, Chris, 143–144

D

Dale, Deirdre, 34–35, 37

Dale, Delores, 40

Dale, Wallace, 35, 37, 41–42

Davis, Don, 65

Davis, Gray, 95

Dead Man Walking (Prejean), 14, 31

Death penalty
    in ancient Greece, 44–46
    changing attitudes toward, 11–14, 17–18
    constitutionality of, 46–47
    constraints on, 72
    current state of, 20–23, 32–33
    declining support for, 61–66, 69
    discrimination in application of, 13–14, 77–78
    future of, 17–18, 69–70
    is a deterrent, 74–79
    is not a deterrent, 12, 24, 29, 80–87
    is uncivilized, 57–60
    mandatory, 30, 52
    mentally ill should not be subject to, 109–112
    moratorium on, 13, 28
    Navajo and, 34–42
    opponents. *see* Abolitionists
    political support for, 29
    as reasoned moral response, 53–54
    reduction in use of, 107–108
    reevaluation of, 16–17, 20–33
    research on, 81–82
    as retribution, 30, 43–56
    should be allowed for juveniles, 100–104
    supporters of, 12, 17–18, 44
    terrorism and, 85–87
    unfair administration of, 23–24, 89–99, 119–123
    See also Executions

Death penalty attorney, viewpoint of, 119–123

Death Penalty Moratorium Implementation Project, 16

Death penalty system
    discrimination in, 13–14, 23–24, 77–78
    flaws in, 13–16, 26–28

Death row inmates
    appellate rights of, 98
    families of, 121–122
    innocent, 14–15, 26, 63–64
    reflections by, 148–158

Death-qualified jurors, 106, 135

Decency, evolving standards of, 13, 49, 101

Defense attorneys
    incompetent, 16, 27–28, 71, 93, 95–96
    mandating adequate, 99

Democrats, support for death penalty among, 29
Demosthenes, 48
Deterrence
  death penalty is a, 74–79
  death penalty is not a, 12, 24, 29, 80–84, 85–87
  research on, 75–78
  of terrorism, 85–87
Dezhbakhsh, Hashem, 77
Discrimination, in application of death penalty, 13–14, 23–24, 77–78
DNA testing, establishing innocence through, 65, 69
Dow, David R., 119
DuBois, Kathleen, 141
Dulles, Trop v. (1958), 49

E

Eastlack, John, 129–147
Eddlem, Thomas R., 100
Effective Death Penalty Act (EDPA), 90, 97
Egeberg, Gary, 124
Ehrlich, Isaac, 76
Eighth Amendment, 13, 21, 49, 100–101
Elliott, David, 98
Emotions, 54–56
Equal protection under law, 50
Equity, 55–56
Erroneous convictions, 14–15, 26, 63–64, 89–90
Executions
  as closure, 30–31
  decline in, 10
  increases in, 21
  of juveniles, 32, 106–107
  of mentally ill, 32, 96–97, 106–107

  methods, 57–60
  moratoriums on, 10, 15–17, 20–21, 76–77
Exile, 46

F

Fairness, 55–56
Family members
  closure for, 30–31, 41–42
  of murderers, 121–122, 129–147
Fetal alcohol syndrome (FAS), 143–144
Fourteenth Amendment, 103–104
Freedman, David, 82
French, Colleen, 141
Furman v. Georgia (1972), 13, 52, 61, 69

G

Gartner, Rosemary, 83
Gas, 58
Gay marriage, 69–70
Georgia, Furman v. (1972), 13, 52, 61, 69
Ginsburg, Ruth Bader, 62–63
Goertzel, Ted, 80
Goodman, Amy, 148
Gordon, Bruce, 157
Gospel, 126–127
Great Depression, 12
Grief, 140
Guided discretion, 25
Guzek, Oregon v. (2006), 64

H

Hanging, 57
Hanna, John, 138
Hatch, Orrin, 80, 83
Hawkins, Steve, 91

Heraclitus, 47, 52
Hernandez, Alex, 14
Hill, Clarence, 65–66
Hill v. McDonough (2006), 65–66
Holmes, Robb, 141
Holmes v. South Carolina (2006), 64
Homer, 44–45
Homicides
    by African Americans, 77–78
    moral differences among, 47–48
    rates of, 75–76, 82–83
    types of, 45–48
House v. Bell (2006), 64
Human dignity, 44
Human rights, international laws on, 31–32
Humanism, 50

I

Illinois
    commutation of sentences in, 10
    moratorium on executions in, 15–16
Incorporation doctrine, 104
Indian reservations, violence on, 35–37
Ingall, Joe, 97
Innocence Project, 64
Innocence Protection Act (2001), 27
Innocent people, sentenced to death penalty, 14–15, 26, 63–65
International Covenant on Civil and Political Rights, 32
International human rights law, 31–32
International opinion, 16, 57, 101–103

Iran, 57
Isonomia, 50

J

Jaffe, D. J., 112
John Paul II (pope), 14
Judicial activism, 103–104
Juries
    death penalty decisions by, 91–92, 105–108
    intuition of, 55–56
Jurisprudence, 52–53
Justice
    as interest of the stronger, 50
    moral, 53–55
    punitive, 39
    rationality and, 51–52
    transcendent concept of, 53
Juvenile death penalty
    should be allowed, 100–104
    Supreme Court on, 68–69
Juvenile offenders, execution of, 32, 106–107

K

Kansas v. Marsh (2006), 62–63, 64–65
Kennedy, Anthony, 62, 66, 68–69
Kentucky, Stanford v. (1989), 101
Klosterman, Chuck, 113
Kroll, Michael, 114

L

Law
    equal protection under, 50
    limits of the, 54–55
Lawal, Amina, 57–58
Lethal injection, 58–60, 65–66
Liebman, James, 16, 92–96, 99
Lindberg, John, 142–143, 146–147

Linderoff, Dave, 89

Lyle, Ellen Hobbs, 59

M

Marsh, Kansas v. (2006), 62–63, 64–65

Marshall, Lawrence C., 15

Mauro, Tony, 61

McDonnell, Thomas, 85

McDonough, Hill v. (2006), 65–66

McManus, Walter, 83084

McVeigh, Timothy, 23

Meditation, 126

Mentally ill persons
    execution of, 32, 96–97, 106–107
    should not be subject to death penalty, 109–112

Mentally retarded persons, execution of, 106–107

Mitigating circumstances, 89–93, 97, 139, 147

Moral development, 127–128

Moral intuitions, 55–56

Moral justice, 53–55

Moral relativity, 47

Morality, 11–13, 48–49

Moussaoui, Zacarias, 85–86, 87

Murder Victim Families for Reconciliation (MVFR), 31

Murderers
    forgiveness for, 124–128
    moral development of, 127–128
    motives of, 50
    viewpoint of mother of, 129–147

Murders. *See* Homicides

N

National Coalition to Abolish the Death Penalty, 31

National Conference on Wrongful Convictions and the Death Penalty, 15

Navajo justice, 38–39

Navajo Nation, rejection of death penalty by, 34–42

Navajo reservation, violence on, 35–37

Nesbitt, Ed, 134, 136–137

New York, 10, 82

Nigeria, 57–58

9/11 attacks, 86, 87

Nonlivestock Animal Humane Death Act, 59–60

Norgard, Katherine, 129

Nuland, Sherwin B., 59

O

O'Connor, Sandra Day, 25–26, 54, 62, 68–69

Oklahoma, Thompson v. (1998), 102

Old Testament, 46

Oliphant, Thomas, 102

On Crimes and Punishment (Beccaria), 11–12

Oregon v. Guzek (2006), 64

P

Pancuronium bromide, 58–59

Pavulon, 58–59

Pericles, 50

Peterson, Scott, 45

Plato, 53, 54

Ponsor, Michael A., 26

Poor inmates, 14

Porter, Anthony, 15

Potassium chloride, 59

Powell, Lewis F., 25

Prayer, 126

Prejean, Helen, 14, 31

Prison chaplain, viewpoint of, 124–128

Progress, 49–50

Prosecutorial misconduct, 16

Prosecutors, decision to seek death penalty by, 107

Protagoras, 49

Protess, David, 15

Psychotics, 110–111

Public opinion
changing, toward death penalty, 11–14, 17–18
consultation with, 48
supporting death penalty, 23

Punitive justice, 39

Pythagoras, 51, 53

R

Racism, in application of death penalty, 13–14, 23–24, 77–78

Rationality, 51–52

Reconciliation, 31

Redemption, 151

Rehnquist, William, 72

Reno, Janet, 80, 83

Republicans, support for death penalty among, 29

Retribution
in Bible, 11
death penalty as, 30, 43–56
rationality and, 51–52
urge for, 44–45

Revenge, 51

Roberts, John, Jr., 66, 67, 72

Roper v. Simmons (2005), 100–101, 103, 106–107

Rubin, Paul H., 74

Rush, Benjamin, 12

Ryan, Carla, 138, 142, 144

Ryan, George
commutations by, 10, 17, 22
moratorium on executions by, 15–16

S

Same-sex marriage, 69–70

Sanders, Brown v. (2006), 64

Satel, Sally, 109

Scalia, Antonin, 52, 64–65, 68, 100–103

Scheck, Barry, 64

Scheidegger, Kent, 62, 93

Schendel, Leah, 94

Scholl, William, 134, 139, 143

Sellin, Thorsten, 75–76, 81–82

Sentencing decisions
arbitrariness in, 13
research on, 24–25

Sentencing errors, 89–99

Shepherd, Joanna Mehlop, 77

Simmons, Christopher, 101

Simmons, Roper v. (2005), 100–101, 103, 106–107

Sloan, Virginia, 63

Snell, Marilyn Berlin, 34

Socrates, 47, 48

Sodium thiopental, 59

Solon, 46

Sophists, 47, 48

Souter, David, 62–63

South Carolina, Holmes v. (2006), 64

South, support for death penalty in, 24

Stanford v. Kentucky (1989), 101

State constitutional amendments, 69–70

State laws, incorporation doctrine and, 104
Stevens, John Paul, 62–63
Stoning, 57–58
Suicide bombers, 86
Supreme Court
    decisions by, 25–26, 61–66
    influence of international opinion on, 101–103
    may alter stance on death penalty, 67–72
    See also specific cases

T

Tennessee, 59–60
Texas, 23, 82
Thompson, Thomas, 143–145
Thompson v. Oklahoma (1998), 102
Thrasymachus, 50
Tompkins, Phillip, 94
Trentacosta, Nick, 90
Trop v. Dulles (1958), 49
Tucker, Karla Faye, 14, 116

U

Unconstitutional laws, retroactive application of, 91
United Nations Convention on the Rights of the Child, 102
Universal Declaration of Human Rights, 12

U.S., Weems v. (1910), 49
Utilitarians, 48

V

Vasquez, Daniel B., 156
Verrilli, Donald, 63
Virginia, Atkins v. (2002), 17, 102, 107

W

Warren, Earl, 49
Weems v. U.S. (1910), 49
Williams, Dobie Gillis, 89–90
Williams, Stanley, 116, 148–158
Williford, Kaykynn, 110
Wittes, Benjamin, 67
Wolff, Michael A., 105
World War I, 12
Wotton, Henry, 57
Wrongful convictions, 14–15, 26, 63–64, 89–90

Y

Yates, Andrea, 109–110, 112
Yazzie, Herb, 36

Z

Zawada, Tom, 136–137, 143, 145, 146